EMBOD

Peter Dodson is Team ... Ministry, and a well-known retreat conductor and spiritual director. He is the author of *Contemplating the Word*, a practical handbook to contemplation, which was acclaimed as 'the most helpful book for someone beginning to discover the contemplative way of prayer.'

Also by Peter Dodson
CONTEMPLATING THE WORD

PETER DODSON

EMBODY THE WORD

Being a Temple of the Holy Spirit

TRi∆NGLE

First published 1989
Triangle
SPCK
Holy Trinity Church
Marylebone Road
London NW1 4DU

British Library Cataloguing in Publication Data

Dodson, Peter, 1932–
    Embody the word.
    1. Christian life. Prayer
    I. Title
    248.3'2

ISBN 0-281-04412-0

Photoset by Rowland Phototypesetting Ltd
Bury St Edmunds, Suffolk
Printed in Great Britain by
Hazell, Watson and Viney Ltd.
Member of BPCC plc
Aylesbury, Bucks

TO MY WIFE, ANN,
who wrestles creatively with the Word
– and with me.

ACKNOWLEDGEMENTS

I bless God for SPCK's editor, Philip Law, who invited and encouraged me to write 'Contemplating the Word'; for those many, many people who read it and found that it spoke, sometimes profoundly, to them; and for those who offered constructive criticism which proved invaluable as I struggled to write this second book.

CONTENTS

The heavenly Father speaks one Word and that he speaks eternally and in this Word he expends all his might: his entire God-nature he utters in this Word . . . This Word lies hidden in the soul unnoticed and beyond our ken, and were it not for rumours in the ground of hearing we should never heed it: but all sounds and voices have to cease and silence, perfect stillness, reign.

JOHANN ECKHART

The word of God is quick, and powerful, and sharper than any two-edged sword.

THE LETTER TO THE HEBREWS

Come, and let [yourself] be built . . . into a spiritual Temple.

THE FIRST LETTER OF PETER

PREFACE

Dear Reader

This book is full of words. Most of those words are mere patter, intended to serve one purpose only: to enable you to appreciate something of *the* Word – the Word spoken by God to his people through the Bible, through Moses and the prophets, the 'wisdom' writings, the Psalms, and above all and pre-eminently through Christ who *is* the Word.

Each chapter begins and, in shorter form, ends with a Word of God – a Word for you to ponder in silence; a Word to cut, as fine as a scalpel, to your innermost being;[1] a Word to give you new heart;[2] a Word by which to live and move and have your being;[3] a Word to enable you to adore God, not only for what he does, but because he is who he is.

Embody the Word is primarily designed for you to use on your own, although each chapter could easily be adapted for use with a group. Before you do either, it would be profitable, even essential, to read or re-read my first book *Contemplating the Word*,[4] especially chapter 5 on 'Becoming Still and Attentive',[5] chapter 6 on 'Distractions, Negative and Positive'[6] and, if you are to lead a group, chapter 7 on 'Listen to MY Words'.[7] Chapter 7 would indicate how each contemplative prayer *group* exercise is intended to last for one hour and is best divided into three twenty-minute sections relating successively to the mind, the heart and the will – to the biblical setting and meaning of the Word, its relationship to personal and group experience, and as a vehicle for living by the Word,[8] especially in terms of intercession and witness.

The prayer exercises in *this* book are not laid out in the extended style. Nevertheless, the three elements referred to in the previous paragraph are always present.

You may be the sort of person who will want initially to read this book straight through. I have written it not so much to be read as to be *worked*. Try to stay with each chapter *daily* for at least a month before moving on to the next. *Any* Word of God is food for a lifetime and more than a lifetime.

But however you decide to use this book, I hope you will be enabled to hear the voice of God 'in all its might and majesty'[9] and, to borrow some words from St Bernard of Clairvaux, to experience the Word as 'honey in the mouth, music in the ear, a shout of gladness in the heart.'[10]

Peter Dodson
November 1988

Come to ME and rest

Come to ME all who labour and are heavy laden, and I will give you rest. Take MY yoke upon you, and learn from ME; for I AM gentle and lowly in heart, and you will find rest for your souls. For MY yoke is easy, and MY burden is light

(MATTHEW 11.28–30, RSV)

These words are found only in the Gospel according to Matthew. They represent something of the author's portrait of Jesus.

The apocryphal book known as Ecclesiasticus, or 'The Wisdom of Jesus Son of Sirach', ends with very similar language: 'Come to me . . . lodge in my house of learning . . . bend your neck to the yoke, be ready to accept discipline; you need not go far to find it. See for yourselves how little were my labours compared to the great peace I have found.'[1]

Matthew links together, more than any of the other three Gospels, the Old and New Testaments. No other New Testament writing so clearly presents Jesus as the fulfilment of 'the law and the prophets'.[2]

The words 'Come to ME . . .' were probably originally intended for the Jewish community in Galilee. The people 'who labour and are heavy laden' might have been those Jews who found the *Torah* or 'Law', as taught by the Pharisees, impossible to keep. To be under 'the yoke of the Law' implied that the Law was heavy going, both for those searching for truth, and for those seeking to ease their conscience. 'The yoke of the Law' was a crushing burden of endless and rigid rules and regulations.

1

Jesus said to those who were worn out by fruitless seeking: 'Come to ME . . . and I will give you rest. Take MY yoke upon you'; from MY life and teaching, you will discover that obedience to the will of God is achieved, *not* so much by the keeping of rules, but by the response of a gentle and humble heart. 'I AM gentle and humble-hearted'; and I set the pattern for you to follow.[3]

How does all this relate to your personal experience? What burdens do you carry? In what ways do you feel crushed? It may be old age, anxiety, responsibility, sickness, disability. Or perhaps you are hooked on drugs, alcohol, cigarettes, spending, sex. Or possibly, you are sick to death of something in your own nature – something in your attitudes or behaviour.

The words of Jesus can cut their way into the middle of your troubled mind and heart: 'Come to ME . . . and I will give you rest.'

The contemplative experience is that these words are full of spirit and life; that they have the power to get under our skin, to penetrate our inner being; that they can enable us to find relief from the burdens we carry, to achieve a profound state of rest.

Find a place in which to be comparatively still and quiet. Sit in a comfortable position, relaxed and alert.[4] Recall the text: 'Come to ME . . . and I will give you rest.' Then bring to mind any particular burden you may be carrying at this point in your life. Take time and care over this. Bring the whole matter out into the open, ready for exposure to the Word.

This may be an easy or a difficult thing to do. Our job is to

> recall whatever in our life causes us most anxiety or pain, so that we may find rest or relief from these our heaviest burdens . . . The mere recollection of our burdens in such a context may bring instant relief. Or it may not. The

burdens may be of such a kind that considerable effort will be needed to recollect them clearly . . . Some of us try to suppress them. Others seek distraction from them. Others try to argue themselves into ignoring them. These and other habitual attempts to cope with burdens by ignoring them in any way . . . may well prevent us from clearly recollecting them. We may therefore have to *force* ourselves to do so at first, even at the cost of pain.[5]

'If', as St John put it, 'we say we have no sin, we deceive ourselves, and there is no truth in us.'[6]

However much you may fret, struggle and resist, you *need* to bring your burdens out into the daylight, to face up to them, and to *accept* them completely: 'There they are,' you might say. 'All the muddle, all the distortion and deception, out into the open – open and exposed.'[7]

You do not have to be too detailed in your recollection, or to wallow in self-pity or self-disgust. Having recollected your burdens as clearly as possible, turn your whole attention to the Word of Christ. Allow the words 'Come to ME . . . and rest' to bathe you, saturate you, and to nourish your whole being. As you give yourself up to the spirit of these life-giving words, you are almost bound to find yourself distracted by all manner of thoughts and feelings. You may therefore find it helpful to do one, or more, or *all* of several things:

1. Repeat the words 'Come to ME . . . and rest' silently, mentally, each time you breathe in. Do it slowly and rhythmically until the words become the rhythm of your life.
2. Repeat the words silently or in the lowest possible whisper, with the lips, as if to get the taste of them in order to chew them over and to digest them fully.
3. Use a string of beads or a rope with a series of

knots. The Orthodox Church has taught us a great deal about the value of beads or knots as an aid to silent prayer. Prayer beads or ropes come in a wide variety of forms.

> Most commonly there are 100 beads or knots, sometimes divided into groups of ten, or else of twenty-five or fifty . . . Personally . . . although I make use of a prayer rope, I take no notice of any subdivision between the knots. The purpose of the prayer rope, as I understand it, is not to measure the number of times the [prayer] is said, for this is not in itself important. But the use of the prayer rope, by giving the hands something to do, helps to aid concentration. Also the movement of the knots or beads through the hands assists a regular and rhythmical recitation.[8]

4. Use a visual focus to remind you of the presence of Christ and of his strong love for you. The words 'Come to ME . . . ' are spoken out of an immense desire and longing for your well-being.

If you stand within the Church's Catholic tradition, you may feel at home with the reserved sacrament as a focus of Christ's presence; or a crucifix; or an icon;[9] or candles. Or, if you are more at home within the Evangelical tradition, you may prefer the simplicity of a plain cross; or a Christian picture. Some people find the 'empty chair' helpful. Put an empty chair near your place of prayer, perhaps facing towards you. Anthony de Mello who developed this particular exercise, is very direct:

> Try this exercise yourself right now, even though at first it might seem childish to you:
> Imagine you see Jesus sitting close to you. In doing this you are putting your imagination at the service of your faith. Jesus isn't here in the way you

4

are imagining him, but he certainly is here and your imagination helps to make you aware of this . . .[10]

No two people are alike. Only you can know how many aids to prayer you need at this point in your life. I tend to be such a distracted person that I need all the help I can get! I sometimes need simultaneously to fix my eyes on a crucifix propped on an empty chair, to breathe the Word in, to whisper it with my lips, *and* to move my prayer beads gently through my fingers! At the other extreme, I am occasionally able to let go of all aids, including the 'words' themselves, and simply to know myself to be at rest in God.

At first, all this may seem very mechanical. It is! Learning to drive a car is initially a matter of getting used to the mechanics, until they become second nature to us.

It is when prayer becomes *merely* mechanical that we act as robots and not as people.

There is a mechanical element in everything we do – for example, in walking down the road. The totterings of a child indicate that the mechanics have not yet been grasped. Yet walking is not *merely* mechanical. We walk as people, not as zombies.

So long as another element is always present – in the case of prayer the intention or the desire to pray – the mechanical basis . . . is not a matter for concern, nor does it become so when the attention to the words fluctuates, as it will surely do.

The important thing is that the intention to pray remains, ourselves meanwhile attending gently to the words as the Holy Spirit enables us, knowing that the heart remains at prayer even though the mind may wander from time to time.[11]

What more can I say at this point? If what I have so far written makes sense to you, all you can do is get on with the work – *be* still and silent; *be* relaxed and attentive; recall the words of Jesus; bring to mind your present burdens; and then for, say, up to twenty minutes, hang on to the words 'Come to ME . . . and rest', for all your life is worth. Let the Word penetrate and saturate your whole being – your mind, your heart, and your will. Let the spirit of the Word live and move and have its being, in *you*:

'Come to ME . . . and rest.'

(*Silence*)

Now gently turn your attention to the work of intercession. If the Word is truly making its home in you, it will do something to the way you perceive other people and the world. If you are beginning to value the experience of coming to Christ to find your rest in him, and in so far as the Word has become embodied in you, you will inevitably become a channel or sign of the Word. The spirit and life of that Word will breed in you a desire that other people, all humankind and all creation, should come to him and rest in him.[12]

At first, your desire may be lukewarm, limited perhaps to one or two close relatives or friends. But as you allow the Word more and more to live in you – as you allow it to root, grow and bear abundant fruit,[13] so you will develop a *burning* desire, aching and longing for the well-being of everyone and everything. But though you may be filled and even overwhelmed with the *general* desire that 'every kind of thing will be well',[14] it is vital that you should channel the Word to *particular* people and situations. Here are a few well-tried hints:

1. Use a current news publication. Take one page only and scan it carefully. Settle for *one* report which reflects the way in which human beings or the world of nature generally, carries a crushing burden. Taking time and care, silently allow the whole scene to become, as far as possible, real and present to you. Silently, gently, lovingly bathe it all in the Word you have received: 'Come to ME . . . and rest.'

2. Keep all postcards sent to you, including the rude ones and comical ones.[15] File them in an appropriate card-index box. The index may be alphabetical, or according to the months of the year and/or days of the week. When you come to the intercessory part of your prayer, take out one postcard at a time. Finger it, read it, recall the person who sent it. Make that person real and present to you: their features, dress, mannerisms, home and family, work setting, etc. If you are awake and alive to that person, you will know the ways in which he or she feels weighed down and crushed. Again, silently and lovingly bathe that person in the light of the Word you have received, 'Come to ME . . . and rest', sharing as far as you can at this stage, something of the Lord's immense and burning desire for that person's well-being.

3. Have a regular weekly scheme for particular intercessions. For example:

   Monday. The members of your immediate family: parents, husband, wife, children, grandchildren.

   Tuesday. The church congregation of which you are a member: the minister(s), adults, children.

   Wednesday. The wider church, especially those Christians you know personally.

Thursday. Other religions: Buddhists, Hindus, Sikhs, Muslims. These days, you may well have a local 'temple' relating to one or more of these, as well as adherents living in your own street or locality. The Word you have received is a *universal* Word, for people of all religions or none.

Friday. The local community: its civic, commercial, industrial, social, cultural life. Again, as far as possible, give the Word not only to community life in *general*, but to those *particular* people you know – people who perhaps carry a crushing burden of responsibility. (You may find it helpful, on a Friday, habitually to hear the Word spoken and channelled from the heart of the Cross).

Saturday. The world and the universe. St Paul reminds us that 'Up to the present . . . the whole created universe groans in all its parts as if in the pangs of childbirth.'[16] It is certainly true that all humanity is labouring under a variety of crushing burdens, political, economic, ecological, racial, and so on.

For all these Monday to Saturday intercessions, it is best to keep a loose-leaf book, so that out-of-date prayer material can be easily extracted and new pages inserted.

Sunday. Take all for whom you have prayed throughout the week – your family, congregation, wider church, other religions, local community, the world and the universe into your Sunday worship, especially into Eucharistic worship. If there are certain people or matters you feel should be included in the public thanksgiving or intercessions, tell the presiding or officiating person.

These various aids to disciplined intercession may or may not be helpful to you. Lists of people and events are not to everyone's taste. You may be content simply to remain in silence and allow the spirit of the indwelling Word to identify the people and things you pray for. When I pray in this way, for example, a particular person will come, often unexpectedly, to the forefront of my mind. I allow that person to become fully present to me and then speak the Word silently and directly to that person. Sometimes, certain images will present themselves to the conscious mind – joyful or sorrowful images – images of God, or of humanity at its best or worst. Often, I will have the strong impression, as I sit in silence with open hands and with the Word burning to get out,[17] that I am holding the whole of our planet. It is about the size of a soccer ball, and I hold it in my hands just as though someone has thrown it to me and I have caught it. Sometimes that globe is full of light and joy; sometimes heavy with sorrow; sometimes a great mixture of tears and laughter. Whichever way it happens to be at any given moment, the Word is always and inevitably direct, clear and relevant. The words 'Come to ME . . . and rest', for example, are as valid for a happy child of God as for a sorrowful one. The Lord extends his arms, so to speak, to both distressed *and* contented people.

Whatever system you choose to help you pray for other people and for the world, when you have completed your intercession time, always end with a brief prayer of personal thanksgiving and dedication. For example:

> Lord, I have listened to your Word.
> Your Word is truth. Your Word is life.
> Help me always to act upon your Word. Amen.[18]

As you leave your prayer time, take the Word, in its shortened form, into every part of your daily life and work. Write this 'Watchword'[19] boldly on, say, two or three cards, one for the kitchen, office or workbench, one for the pocket or handbag, and, if you own a car, one for the dashboard. A small cross or crucifix might be a useful alternative or addition to the Word-card. Or you might like to carry prayer beads or rope (mine are always either on my prayer table or in my cassock pocket), so that you may be able to handle them at any or every odd moment, enabling you to recall the Watchword for yourself and others. In this way, the Word becomes increasingly embodied in you, affecting your attitudes and relationships in every waking and sleeping moment. You become a *doer* of the Word as well as a hearer.[20] The Word does something to the way you are – quickly or slowly, obviously or imperceptibly. The change may of course be more noticeable to other people than to yourself. But embodying the Word is not primarily about personal wholeness and holiness. It is about co-operating with the Word and Will of God – about being an instrument or channel or sign of his saving Word and Will.

The principles and practice outlined in this chapter apply to *all* the other chapters in this book. In fact, there is sound sense in beginning *every* contemplative exercise by silently recalling the loving command to 'Come to ME . . . and rest', and by remembering, facing and accepting the burdens of the moment. This need take no longer than a couple of minutes, enabling you to be better prepared to hear, receive, embody and live by whichever Word has been particularly selected for contemplation.

'Come to ME . . . and rest.'

Consider your life

'Consider your way of life.'
(HAGGAI 1.5)

This is a prophetic Word. It was uttered through a man named Haggai, in Jerusalem, about 2,500 years ago. Like all authentic prophecy, it speaks directly, clearly, incisively to you and to me: 'Consider your way of life.'

Other English versions of the Scriptures translate the same Hebrew text in a different way: for example, 'Reflect carefully how things have gone for you', 'Don't you see what is happening to you?', 'Give careful thought to your ways.'[1]

For silent contemplation, be free to use whichever version speaks most clearly to *you*. I was moved to select 'Consider your way of life' for three reasons: first, because it makes the clearest and most incisive sense to *me*; secondly, because it is among the shortest of the various versions, only five words instead of six or eight; and thirdly, because, as we shall see, it can be more easily shortened even further. For contemplation, the shorter the phrase the better.

Before getting down to the work of contemplating this particular Word, it is important, as I stressed in my introduction, to see it in its biblical context and relationship to the Christian tradition, and to understand it in terms of our own experience.

Old Testament history tells us that in the year 536 BC, the Jews, who had been living in exile in Babylon, were able to return to Palestine. According to the prophet Ezra, the first thing they did was to set up an altar:

> The Israelites now being . . . assembled as one man in Jerusalem . . . Jeshua son of Jozadak and his fellow priests, and Zerubbabel son of Shealtiel and his kinsmen, set to work and built the altar of the God of Israel . . . They put the altar in place first . . .[2]

The following year they laid the foundation of the Temple:

> They appointed Levites . . . to supervise the work of the House of the Lord . . . When the builders had laid the foundation of the temple . . . they chanted praises and thanksgiving to the Lord, singing, 'It is good to give thanks to the Lord, for his love . . . endures for ever.'[3]

Having laid the foundation, the work of Temple building came to a stop. The site remained a wasteland for a period of fifteen years. The rebuilding work was suspended for two reasons: the Jews refused the co-operation of 'semi-pagans' who had colonized the north of Palestine; and the Jews themselves, perhaps influenced by disillusioned priests, Levites and other leading figures, simply lost interest.

It seems the Jews were primarily and busily engaged in working on their own homes, a self-centred pre-occupation which proved to be a recipe for disaster.

Enter Haggai:

> The word of the Lord came through the prophet Haggai to Zerubbabel . . . governor of Judah, and to Joshua . . . the high priest: These are the words of the Lord of hosts: This nation says to itself that it is not yet time for the Temple of the Lord to be rebuilt . . . Is it a time for you to live in your own well-roofed houses, while this Temple lies in ruins? . . . Consider your way of life. You have sown much but reaped little; you eat but never as much as you wish, you

drink but never more than you need, you are clothed but never warm, and the labourer puts his wages into a purse with a hole in it . . . Consider your way of life . . .[4]

If you own a Good News Bible, turn to the book of Haggai. There you will find a simple line drawing which makes Haggai's point exactly: well-built houses surrounding a Temple which is nothing but a ruin. The city and the nation had lost its soul. The Temple, which was meant to be the heart, centre, pivot and source of well-being for the whole city and nation, lay ruined, neglected, ignored.

Can we see ourselves in any of this? The story of the Jews, and especially of the Temple, is your story and my story – the story of every human being who has ever lived or ever will live. But for the moment, I want to cut a long story short and get to the point clearly made in the *New* Testament: *you* are the Temple. St Paul wrote in his letters to the Christians of Corinth: 'Surely you know that you are God's temple, where the Spirit of God dwells . . .'; 'Don't you know that your body is the temple of the Holy Spirit . . . ?' More crucially, the Gospel according to John says of Jesus: 'The temple he was speaking of was his body.'[5]

You are the Temple, not some special bit of you, but the *whole* of you: the whole thinking, feeling, striving flesh and blood human being which is you.

It is here that the fine, sharp,[6] prophetic Word, spoken through Haggai, cuts in: 'Consider your way of life.'

You may be lucky enough to have a decent roof over your head. You may even have spent a great deal of time, energy, skill and money on house and garden. That does not necessarily lead to a sense of personal (or family!) well-being. Evidence suggests that the lives of people who live in this way are often the most empty, and in the greatest state of neglect and ruin. I know, for example, of one married couple in their middle forties. They have a fine, spacious, beautifully furnished bungalow, an expensive car and river launch. They are deeply in debt, are both drinking heavily, and are constantly violent towards each other. You may not have reached that kind of extreme, but the vital question remains: what kind of a temple are *you*, at this point in your life?

One thing I can say with absolute certainty: you are not a *perfect* temple. If you are able even to begin to face the truth, you are bound to recognize in yourself, whatever the reasons may be, something of a sad, sinful and sorry mess: something of a muddled mind, hardened heart and weakened will; something of apathy and disregard of that which is central, pivotal and the source of well-being for all authentic human living. Depending on the level of your perception, you may even be able to see yourself as nothing but a wasted ruin of a person, as a complete sham, however well early foundations may have been laid.

The Lord speaks to you. He says, 'Consider your way of life.' This is not a mere invitation to be accepted or refused, although of course you *can* refuse and hang the consequences! These words of God have the imperative strength of a direct command.[7] They are spoken out of God's burning love and desire for your well-being. They are the words of a loving Father to a child in danger: words that need to cut, burn, filter their way into your stubborn, rebellious human nature; words that need to be 'fleshed out', embodied, incarnated in you.

The cutting edge of the Lord's words spoken through Haggai, can become even more incisive, searching and probing, if they can be heard coming, so to speak, from the lips of Jesus. This is, by the way, the best measure of the truth and power of *any* Old

Testament Word.[8] In some of my own times of silent contemplation, this particular Word has spoken starkly, lovingly, tenderly from the heart of a crucifix. It is at such moments that, for example, the poetry of St John of the Cross begins to make sense to me:

> Oh flame of love so living,
> How tenderly you force
> To my soul's inmost core your fiery probe![9]

'Consider your way of life', says the crucifix to me. 'Consider your life in the light of the love you see in ME. I AM the perfect Temple. I did not abandon or neglect the work God gave ME to do. I did it to perfection. I did it until I could do no more, even if it meant that I was to die doing it.' The living flame of his love makes me see that although there *is* an Altar and Temple foundation of love somewhere in me, I am guilty of the most appalling apathy, neglect, ignorance. By comparison to the love I see in the Cross of Christ, I am a ruin of a man and need to take a good look at my life. I need to examine myself thoroughly, especially in the light and heat of the love that radiates from the Cross.

What more do I need to say at this point? My job is to encourage you to be still, silent, relaxed, in order to give total attention to the Word spoken through Haggai, using perhaps one, or more, or all of the aids outlined in Month One (pp. 3–5) to cease articulation of thoughts and feelings, and simply to hang on to the Word in the silence, for all your life is worth – to let the spirit and life of the Word speak to the very middle of your being, so that it may root, grow, burst into flower and bear fruit,[10] in you.

As you allow this to happen, you may find it helpful to shorten 'Consider your way of life' to, say, 'Consider your life'. The shorter the phrase the better.

You may also benefit from hearing your own name added to this Word.[11] For example, when I am contemplating this Word, the food for my silence is: 'Peter, consider your life.'

So, 'Be still . . .', 'Be silent . . .', 'Let the word of Christ dwell in you richly . . .'[12]

'(Name), consider your life.'

(*Silence*)

The more you contemplate this Word in silence, the more its spirit and life will impregnate your whole being. It will have an accumulative effect. It will *do* something to the way you think and feel and behave. Bit by bit, you will find yourself becoming more conscious of and sensitive towards the power of the Word and the love of God it conveys, not only to you, but to other people, to the world and all creation. If this Word is truly making its home in you, you will increasingly find yourself caught up in sharing something of God's immense desire and longing for the well-being of everyone and everything that exists.

With this particular Word, you will inevitably find yourself in touch with life's sorrowful mysteries, with the general and disastrous failure to *be* the Temple of God. The discipline of contemplating this Word will *drive* you to the vital work of intercession. Like Haggai, you will become a channel of this Word, for individual people, for the world and all creation. It will not be *you* doing the intercessory work: it will be the Word, understood in the fullest and richest sense who will be working in you and through you.[13]

For example, using whatever intercession plan seems right for you (see pp. 6–9), suppose you are moved to pray for one particular person, say, a man named Alan who by his own action or inaction, has ruined his life. He is currently serving a prison sentence, his wife is filing for divorce, his teenage children hate him and refuse to visit him. He is a broken man.

Using your imagination, picture him as clearly as you can. Take time and care over this. As far as possible, put yourself inside the skin of that broken, ruined human being. Saturate him with the Word that speaks within and through you: 'Alan, consider your life.'

If you *do* get deeply in touch with that crushed man, you may find yourself caught up in sharing God's own grief, frustration and anger – with the God who says:

> 'How can I bear MY sorrow?
> I AM sick at heart . . .
> I AM wounded at the sight of MY people's wound;
> I go like a mourner, overcome with horror . . .
>
> MY eyes stream with tears,
> ceaselessly, day and night . . .
>
> I drench you with MY tears.'[14]

If that becomes part of your experience, do not inhibit the *expression* of that frustration and anger. Release the energy. Yell it out and cry it out of your system, just as God does. Yell it out again and again, silently or aloud: 'Alan, consider your life! Consider your life!'

Stay with Alan until it becomes clear that you can safely leave him, at least for the present. Offer a brief prayer of thanksgiving to God that the Word has gone forth through you; and then move on to another person, group of persons, or situation. The discipline of contemplative prayer, especially in its intercessory aspect, can flood us with overwhelming joy, the most devastating sorrow, and all shades in between. It is in moments of extremity that we discover that authentic prayer can be very tough indeed. There is agony and ecstacy, crucifixion and resurrection, in sharing God's loving compassion for his people. If the work of intercession does become excruciatingly painful – if in addition, we find it difficult or impossible to release the pain, we may be tempted to run away from it, even to stop praying altogether. If you find yourself falling into such a trap, all I can do is to urge you not to run away, but to stay with the pain of loving. Stay with whatever the Word gives you. Learn from it and grow by it. Running away from pain is not the Christ way or the true contemplative way.

Enough said. My job is to encourage you to get on, now, with the work of intercession, in the light of the Word which is embodying itself in you:

'Consider your life.'

When you have completed your time of intercession, offer a closing prayer of thanksgiving and dedication. You can devise your own prayer. I use a basic structure which I vary from time to time:

> Lord, I bless you and adore you for your Word –
> for your healing, transforming, life-giving Word.
> Your Word is a light to my path.
> Your Word is truth.
> Let it be to me according to your Word. Amen.

I also commend to you a prayer adapted from The Alternative Service Book 1980:

> Almighty God,
> thank you for the gift of your holy Word.

May it be a lantern to my feet,
a light to my path,
and a strength to my life.
Take me and use me to love and serve all humankind
in the power of the Holy Spirit
and in the name of your Son,
Jesus Christ our Lord. Amen.[15]

The more you contemplate 'Consider your life', the more you will become a channel, a sign, a living witness[16] to its spirit and life, for your immediate family, your church congregation, your work colleagues, etc. Keep the Watchword[17] with you at all times and in all places. Let it act as a constant reminder, not only of God's presence and Word to you, but also of the way you are called to be. Allow the Word to keep your attitudes and behaviour in check. To put it in biblical language, live your daily life, every bit of your daily life 'by every word that comes from the mouth of God.'[18] Let 'Consider your life' be and become the motivating power in and through all that you are and all that you do. In this way, your struggle to live an authentic Christian life will be kept continually under review, as it *must* be!

'Consider your life.'

Build a temple to MY glory

Build a Temple acceptable to ME, where I can show MY glory.

(HAGGAI 1.8)

What is a temple? Primarily, a temple is regarded as the dwelling-place or 'house' of God. A temple is further understood to be a place in which to worship God. A primitive temple might take the simple form of a hollow tree in which the image of a god is placed.[1]

Historically, the word 'temple' has always been applied to the sacred buildings of, say, the Egyptians, Greeks and Romans. Today, in Britain, we have become accustomed to Buddhist, Hindu and Sikh temples. In France, Protestant places of worship are called temples, the word *église* (church) being reserved for the predominantly Roman Catholic buildings.

In the Hebrew/Christian tradition, the word 'temple' is especially associated with the city of Jerusalem. Three successive temples were erected in Jerusalem, more or less on the same site.[2] They were the temples of Solomon, Zerubbabel and Herod. Solomon's Temple was destroyed by fire in the early part of the sixth century BC. It was to the building of a *second* temple that the prophet Haggai referred. He addressed himself primarily to Zerubbabel, the governor of Judah, appealing for his leadership: 'These are the words of the Lord . . . : Consider your way of life . . . Build a temple acceptable to ME, where I can show MY glory.'[3]

We know the building work was completed and this second Temple dedicated in 516 BC. But we have

21

little clear idea of its layout or appearance. Scholars suggest it was probably modelled on the ground plan of Solomon's Temple. One thing is certain: although Zerubbabel's Temple was not as glorious as Solomon's, it was nevertheless built, as all 'houses of God' must be, to the glory of God.[4] This is also exciting-ly true of the *New* Testament assertion that '*You* are God's Temple'.[5] If you truly 'consider your way of life', you will begin to recognize your need to 'build a Temple acceptable to ME, where I can show MY glory'.

It is worth recalling here, that the word 'contempla-tion' is itself connected with the word 'temple', which may be defined as an open space in which God does his work. Christian contemplation is precisely about allowing yourself to *be* the Temple – to *be* the open space in which God can live and work.[6]

The discipline of contemplation is a powerful tool, enabling us to 'build upon the foundation laid by the apostles and prophets, [with] Christ Jesus himself [as] the foundation stone. In him the whole structure . . . grows into a holy temple.' In contemplation we are built into a 'spiritual dwelling for God'.[7]

Contemplation *is* the work of temple building. A temple 'acceptable' to God is one in which we actively co-operate with God, in which God is the inspiration and prime mover. All *we* have to do is give God the 'space', not only in terms of time and place, but in terms of an open mind, heart and will. Our active co-operation in this way *is* our obedience to God's command to 'build a temple'. It is *he* who does the work. In fact, as Lady Julian of Norwich perceived centuries ago, 'There is no doer but he'.[8] And long before her, the Psalmist proclaimed 'Unless the Lord builds the house, its builders will have toiled in vain.'[9]

Any temple built to the glory of God is bound to be great and powerful, splendid and majestic. In King

Solomon's day, the Temple stood on the highest point of the city. It was massively built and filled with the costliest furniture and fittings. If you want to catch something of a vision of what it means to be the 'temple of the living God', explore the First Book of Kings, chapters 5 to 7, and possibly also chapters 8 and 9. Solomon inevitably paid special attention to the 'inner sanctuary, the Most Holy Place':

> [Solomon] made . . . all the furnishings for the house of the Lord: the golden altar and the golden table upon which was set the Bread of the Presence; the lamp-stands of red gold, five on the right side and five on the left side of the inner shrine; the flowers, lamps and tongs, of gold; the cups, snuffers, tossing-bowls, saucers, and firepans, of red gold; and the panels for the doors of the inner sanctuary, the Most Holy Place, and for the doors of the house, of gold.[10]

Throughout Christian history, church buildings, especially of the Catholic and Orthodox traditions, have been constructed richly and entirely to the glory of God, with special attention to the sanctuary or 'Most Holy Place'.

You are the Temple. You are to be and become a great and powerful, splendid and majestic 'House of God'. In particular your own 'inner sanctuary' – your own 'Most Holy Place' – is to be a 'heart of gold'.

If, in your times of contemplation, you allow the spirit of 'Build a Temple acceptable to ME, where I can show MY glory' to cut its way to your 'innermost thoughts and desires'[11] – if you allow the spirit of this Word to live at the core of your being, you *will* be built into a holy Temple, and your 'Most Holy Place' will become pure gold. Contemplative experience testifies to the truth of the Psalmist's proclamation: 'The words of the Lord are pure words: silver refined in a crucible, gold seven times purified.'[12] If God has drawn you to long for an 'inner sanctuary' which is pure and good as gold, allow yourself to be filled with the pure gold of his Word. Be disciplined with your times of silent contemplation. Give undivided attention to what God is saying to you. Like a soldier on parade or on the battlefield, listen to the Word of command and obey it. In fact, in biblical teaching, to hear the Word *is* to obey it.[13]

Before you get on with this vital work, think further about 'temple' buildings; not the ones in Jerusalem, but a small building in the centre of the city of York, called St Helen's, of which I am privileged to have oversight. It stands in what has been called 'the busiest tourist area in Europe'. The church building has a clean, bright, welcoming façade. Its light oak doors are open daily. Some of the people who live and work in and around the city, make a habit of entering the building, to be still and quiet, to reflect, meditate, pray – to listen for the voice of God – to gaze at the immaculate sanctuary with its large spotlighted Italian crucifix suspended above the altar, and its candle-lit aumbry indicating the Lord's sacramental presence.

One man, John, an employee of York's phrenetic Post Office, finds his regular visits to St Helen's so 'therapeutic', that he was moved to write to me as follows:

> I thank God for the invaluable and indispensable function served by the beautiful church of St Helen in the busy life of the city of York. In an age when there is such a pronounced and fevered pursuit of self-aggrandisement and selfish gain, it is a rich and wonderful blessing that God has provided a place like St Helen's, where we can be quiet and still and hear his Word speaking to us so gently but persistently in the silence, reminding us of our true

purpose on earth. There are many who share in the lives
of cities everywhere who are daily at the mercy of cruel
and selfish motives, exploitation and domination clothed
in many forms of hypocrisy and cant. The people of our
cities desperately need to know that God loves them; that
compassion, care, humility and service are the values
which abide and which will always matter; that in the face
of all that denies and despises him in this world, God still
reigns and is there offering, inviting and encouraging
love and coping with the rejection of love at all levels
of creation. This is the knowledge I find in the deep
and healing silence of St Helen's, sustaining us all and
maintaining sanity.

A steady stream of tourists also enters the building.
Some leave almost immediately, without so much as a
second glance, as if the silence and stillness is more
than they can bear. Others seem interested only in
things like the architecture, stained glass, organ, or
the photographs of the excellent choir. But many,
many of them, bless God, find it, to quote from the
visitors' book, a 'haven of quiet', an 'oasis of peace', a
place 'just right for contemplation', 'a place of sanity in
a mad, bad world', a place in which to cry 'God help
me!', a place in which 'God is'.

'*You* are the Temple.' Are you open to people? Do
people find in you the stillness and quiet in which to
hear the 'Word speaking . . . gently but persistently
. . . reminding [them] of [their] true purpose on
earth'? Do people see in you a clear sign of the Word
which says, for example, 'Come to ME, all whose work
is hard, whose load is heavy, and I will give you rest
. . . Consider your way of life . . . Build a Temple to MY
glory'? Do people see in you an immaculate inner
sanctuary, a Most Holy Place, a heart of gold? Do they
perceive in you the living presence of the Lord of love?
Do people find in you a 'deep and healing silence', a
'haven', an 'oasis of peace', 'sustaining all and

maintaining sanity', a place to cry for help, a place in which 'God is'?

But St Helen's in York is not *all* silence and stillness. At least three times every week, it is filled with the sound of the spoken voice, of music and of movement, all in response to God's sacrificial love, in 'psalms, hymns and songs; singing and making music in the heart to the Lord',[14] reading, preaching, praying aloud, sharing, offering, consecrating, receiving, blessing.

'*You* are the Temple.' Is there a ready response in you to the Lord of love, in word, song and action? Is there in you the voicing and showing of adoration, praise, thanksgiving, penitence, petition, intercession?

We are beginning to get some clue about temple building – what it means to 'Build a Temple acceptable to ME, where I can show MY glory.'

Do you find the prospect daunting and even frightening? The people of Jerusalem in Haggai's day certainly did. There lay the ruined Temple. The people were faced with the task of rebuilding: 'Zerubbabel . . . Joshua . . . and the rest of the people listened to what the Lord their God had said [through Haggai], and they were filled with fear.'[15]

Some of them could remember the glory of Solomon's Temple. When the foundation of the *second* Temple had been laid, there was 'a great shout of praise to the Lord . . . But many of the priests and Levites and heads of families, who were old enough to have seen the former Temple, wept and wailed.'[16] As I suggested earlier, it was the disillusionment of these more influential people that quickly and adversely affected the general public and led to apathy towards and neglect of the Temple site. Little wonder that the Lord's Word to 'Build . . .' filled them with fear and trepidation.

So Haggai the Lord's messenger, as the Lord had commissioned him, said to the people: I AM with you . . . Zerubbabel, take heart . . . ; take heart, Joshua . . . Take heart, all you people . . . Begin the work, for I AM with you . . . and MY spirit is present among you.[17]

This Word to Zerubbabel, Joshua and all the rest, is also the Lord's Word for you. It is a Word of encouragement and support. As you struggle with your own apathy and neglect – as you struggle with the vision of what it means to *be* the Temple of God – as you struggle with the discipline of con*templa*tion – as you 'begin the work' of temple building, it is with the clear and direct assurance that the Lord is with you and that the building of the temple is achieved by the presence and power of his Spirit.

So, 'Be still . . .', 'Be silent . . .', 'Desire the milk of the Word so that you may grow by it.'[18]

'Build a Temple . . . to . . . MY glory.'

(Silence)

The Word of God, given to us in the Bible, is always addressed either to a nation, to individuals, or to both. This particular Word was originally spoken to 'Zerubbabel, Joshua, and the rest of the people.' Because it is a prophetic and eternal Word – because it is a *true* Word – it always and everywhere has both a personal and a general, universal application. The Word which has spoken to the whole of *your* being, is also a Word for *all* the Zerubbabels and Joshuas of this world, for every single man, woman and child on our planet, and for every last scrap of creation.

We might say that Zerubbabel, the governor of Judah, and Joshua, the high priest, represent the world's secular and religious authorities. It might be appropriate therefore, in your work of intercession, to

channel the Word, especially to those whose responsibility it is to lead local, national and international
communities in the work of temple building. I am not
suggesting you should pray *only* for the secular and
religious leaders, but if *they* have neither the vision nor
the motivation – if, as too often seems to be the case,
our leaders are consciously or unconsciously hell-bent
on the ruination and destruction of our planet, its
people and even of the space beyond our planet – they
need desperately to 'hear, and receive [this] holy
Word.'[19]

You are privileged to be an instrument of God's
loving desire for his creation, and of the spirit and life
of his saving Word: 'You, the leaders of MY people
throughout the world, and you, all MY people; you MY
whole creation, build a Temple acceptable to ME,
where I can show MY glory. Build a holy Temple
in which I can live and work, great and powerful,
splendid and majestic, with a heart of gold. Allow the
pure gold of MY Word to impregnate everyone and
everything. Be a haven of quiet, of peace, of sanity – a
place right for contemplating ME – a place where I AM –
a place full of adoration, praise, thanksgiving and all
other appropriate responses to MY love. Take heart, all
you leaders and people; take heart, MY whole creation.
Take heart and begin the work, for I AM with you and
MY spirit is present among you. Build a Temple to MY
glory.'

As I write this, I sense the same spirit, the same
strong desire and longing, the same power of Christ
the Word, bursting from the pages of Paul's letter to
the Ephesians. For example:

Praise be to the God and Father of our Lord Jesus Christ
. . . In Christ he chose us . . . to be dedicated, to be
without blemish in his sight, to be full of love; . . . He has
made known to us his hidden purpose . . . : namely, that

the universe, all in heaven and on earth, might be brought into a unity in Christ . . . I pray that . . . God . . . may give you . . . wisdom and vision, by which there comes the knowledge of him. I pray that your inward eyes may be illumined, so that you may know the . . . hope . . . wealth and glory . . . he offers you . . . how vast the resources of his power . . . You are built upon the foundation laid by the apostles and prophets, and Christ Jesus himself is the foundation-stone. In him the whole building is bonded together and grows into a holy temple in the Lord. In him you too are being built with all the rest into a spiritual dwelling for God . . . With this in mind, then, [I pray] to the Father . . . that out of the treasures of his glory he may grant you strength and power through his Spirit in your inner being, that through faith Christ may dwell in your hearts with love. With deep roots and firm foundations, may you be strong to grasp . . . what is the breadth and length and height and depth of the love of Christ, and to know it, though it is beyond knowledge. So may you attain to fullness of being, the fullness of God himself.[20]

So far, in this section, I have spoken only of the joyful/painful work of *intercession* in the light of the Word. We neglect this vital work at our peril. But if the Word has truly spoken to mind and heart, it will also provoke responses of adoration, praise, thanksgiving, penitence, petition as well as intercession. In other words, if in silent contemplation the Word has truly become embodied in your human nature, it will inevitably breed praise, thanksgiving, and the desire to grow in love for God, for his people everywhere, for the whole creation.[21]

Think of the inexhaustible richness of the nature and work of God himself, of human nature and activity, and of all creation. As I sit writing at my desk, a beautiful and sweet-natured Alsatian bitch sleeps peacefully at my feet. I look beyond the desk through the window; I see a fence festooned with the 'red gold' of a virginia creeper in autumn. Both are part of the glory of the 'Temple' of God's creation. Both can move me to adoration of God, as well as to praise and thanksgiving.

Next door to the creepered fence, there is a neglected house. Its paintwork has almost disappeared, its garden a great mass of weeds. Old and dirty net curtains hang in shreds at the windows, two panes of which are broken. Only one person in the neighbourhood is able to gain access. I have heard that the house contains one chair, one cat, and one not very elderly lady who lives there as a total recluse. She spends many hours of night and day screaming blasphemies and obscenities, all of which can be heard coming from the broken windows and air bricks. Here is a candidate for intercession – for the sharing of God's desire for her – for the channelling of his penetrating, healing, transforming Word: 'Build a Temple, acceptable to ME, where I can show MY glory.'

In the light of this Word, you will be moved, in your own way and as far as you are able, to respond to the loving God who has spoken his Word to the whole of your being, and to channel its spirit and life to other human beings, situations and events.

'Build a Temple acceptable to ME, where I can show MY glory.' . . .

Lord, I praise you and bless you for your holy Word. Your Word is a light to my path. Your Word is truth. Give me the insight to keep it with all my heart. Amen.[22]

Keep the Watchword with you as you go about your daily work, rest and play. The more you allow the Word to become embodied in you, the more it will affect your attitudes and behaviour. The New Testament Letter of James encourages you to 'Submit to God and accept the word that he plants in your heart, which is able to save you.' The writer then insists that you

> Do not deceive (yourself) by just listening to his word; instead, put it into practice . . . Whoever looks into the perfect law that sets people free, who keeps on paying attention to it and does not simply listen and then forget it, but puts it into practice – that person will be blessed by God in what he does.[23]

Speaking through the prophet Jeremiah, the Lord makes a similar point and refers explicitly to the false use of the Temple:

> You keep saying, 'This place is the temple of the Lord, the temple of the Lord, the temple of the Lord!' This catchword of yours is a lie; put no trust in it. Mend your ways and your doings, deal fairly with one another, do not oppress the alien, the orphan, and the widow.[24]

If you persistently recall and repeat the Watchword, do not allow it to become a lie so that it cannot be trusted. Let it be and become the spring, the drive, the motivating power in and through all that you are and all that you do, especially in active concern and care for people and for the environment.

A clear sign that you are one of those whose hearts God has touched,[25] that the Word is truly making its home in you, that you are being and becoming a glorious Temple, is to be seen in the quality of your care for others, and in your own moral stature. The Letter of James sums it up as follows:

> The kind of religion which is without stain or fault in the sight of God our Father is this: to go to the help of orphans and widows in their distress and keep oneself untarnished by the world.[26]

'Build a Temple . . . to . . . MY glory.'

MY resting-place, MY home, MY desire

This is MY *resting-place for ever; here will I make* MY *home, for such is* MY *desire.*

(PSALM 132.14)

This verse of the Psalms refers to the Temple which stood at the heart of Jerusalem. The words, which are attributed to God, may have been chanted by a Temple priest or cultic prophet.[1]

The Psalms have been regarded and used for many centuries of the Hebrew/Christian tradition as an anthology of religious poems. In several places, they give valuable insights into the way a devout Jew viewed the Temple, the way he addressed himself to the God who had made his home there:

O Lord, I love the beauty of thy house,
   the place where thy glory dwells.

Holiness is the beauty of thy temple.

Happy is the man of thy choice, whom thou dost bring
    to dwell in thy courts;
  let us enjoy the blessing of thy house,
    thy holy temple.

I, through thy great love, may come into thy house,
and bow low toward thy holy temple in awe of thee.

I will bring sacrifices into thy temple
and fulfil my vows to thee.

[People] are filled with the rich plenty of thy house,
   and thou givest them water from the flowing stream of
    thy delights;

for with thee is the fountain of life,
and in thy light we are bathed with light.

Even the sparrow finds a home,
    and the swallow has her nest,
where she rears her brood beside thy altars . . .
Happy are those who dwell in thy house;
    they never cease from praising thee.

O God, we re-enact the story of thy true love
        within thy temple;
    the praise thy name deserves, O God,
        is heard at earth's farthest bounds.[2]

I cannot help but see the Lord taking hold of those
words and changing them into an expression of his
own essential nature. Through those words from the
Psalms I hear him speaking directly, clearly – not to the
Temple in Jerusalem, but to you personally, because
'*You* are the Temple':

You are the Temple. I love the beauty of you, the place
where MY glory dwells. Holiness is the beauty of MY
Temple. Happy the people I choose, whom I bring to
dwell in you; let them enjoy the blessing of MY house, MY
holy Temple. They, through MY great love, may come into
you and bow low towards you in awe of ME. They will
bring sacrifices into you and fulfil their vows unto ME.
People are filled with the rich plenty they find in you, and
I give them water from the flowing stream of MY delights;
for with ME is the fountain of life, and in MY light they are
bathed with light.
    Even the animal world finds a home in you. Happy are
those who dwell in you; they never cease from praising
ME. They re-enact the story of MY true love within you, MY
Temple; the praise MY name deserves is heard at earth's
farthest bounds.

This poses many intriguing and challenging questions which cannot be fully explored in this book.
However, whatever the questions, there is no doubt

that it represents a powerful, positive, affirmative view of your humanity. You are the Temple, loved, beautiful, glorious, holy, enabling people to find happiness, blessing, and humility before the awesomeness of God; and all the rest!

Every single key word and image deserves unwrapping and pursuing. For the moment, I select only the first of them: love.

'I love the beauty of you,' says God. 'People, through MY great love, may come into you.'

The witness of the Scriptures and of the contemplative tradition, is that God burns with love for you and all humankind – that his love is a strong, tender, compassionate love[3] – that he longs for you to 'Make your home in ME, as I make MINE in you'[4] – that he aches for you to hear and receive and live by the Word that comes from his mouth: '[You are] MY resting-place for ever; [in you] I will make MY home, for such is MY desire.'

Your struggle to build a Temple to the glory of God, in which God can rest and make a home, is itself your loving response to God's great love for you.

Let John Ruusbroec speak for all contemplatives when he likens the meeting of God's Spirit with our spirit to a storm of love:

In this storm of love two spirits struggle – the Spirit of God and our spirit. God, by means of the Holy Spirit, inclines himself toward us, and we are thereby touched in love; our spirit, by means of God's activity and . . . power, impels and inclines itself toward God, and thereby God is touched. From these two movements there arises the struggle of love, for in this most profound (and intimate) meeting . . . each spirit is wounded by love. These two spirits, that is, our spirit and God's Spirit, cast a radiant light upon one another and each reveals to the other its countenance. This makes the two spirits incessantly strive after one another in love. Each demands of the other what it is, and each offers to the other and invites it to accept what it is. This makes these loving spirits lose themselves in one another. God's touch and his giving of himself, together with our striving in love and our giving of ourselves in return – this is what sets love on a firm foundation.[5]

How does this talk of love relate to the *anger* of God, to the way he lashes[6] out at people, particularly at those who defile the Temple?

The prophet Malachi represents God as saying to his people 'I love you', and then he rages at them:

> I will lay a curse on you. I will turn your blessings into a curse; yes, into a curse . . . I will . . . fling offal in your faces . . . and I will banish you from MY presence . . . I have made you mean and despicable in the eyes of the people.[7]

The same angry frustration, at the human level, is seen in the Psalms: 'O God, the heathen have set foot in thy domain, defiled thy holy temple.' 'Bitter enemies of thy temple tear me in pieces.'[8]

Jesus blazes with fury and violence towards those who turn the Temple of King Herod into a market place for exploiting visitors.[9] In many other places in the Gospels,

> Jesus allows us to see him truly within the prophetic tradition, forthrightly denouncing those . . . who substitute idolatry for the true religion and thus, not surprisingly, bringing retribution upon himself. Like Jeremiah before him, Jesus felt within himself the fire of God's anger: 'Your anger against them burns in me too, Lord, and I can't hold it in any longer.'[10]

There is no easy answer to the question of violent anger. All I can say here is that it can be used destructively or creatively, and that creative anger is an essential ingredient of God's love and of all authentic human love.

'You are the Temple.' Because God loves you – because he desires the very best for you – because he longs to rest in you and be at home in you, he can rightly be angry over the way you allow yourself or others to abuse and defile you; and *you* can rightly be angry with yourself and with others. If you have begun to catch a glimpse of the kind of Temple you were created to be – if in the light of that vision, you begin to see the extent of the damage and neglect, you will inevitably share, with God, something of angry frustration. You will see the damage and neglect as an enemy and as a mean and despicable curse. You will find yourself, in one way or another, crying out with the Psalmist over the defilement of the holy Temple. In the struggle with the storm and the fire of God's love, you may well find yourself torn in pieces.

Every bit of the struggle is worthwhile – the struggle to become still enough, beautiful, glorious and holy enough, pure and wholesome enough to reflect the face of God – the struggle to be the sort of Temple in which people and all creation will find, for example, happiness, blessing, food, drink, light, home – the struggle to be the place in which God himself can rest and make a home.

'MY resting-place . . . MY home . . . MY desire.'

(*Silence*)

As we have seen, this Word of God was probably proclaimed through a priest or prophet, to those who came to worship in the Temple at Jerusalem: 'This is MY resting-place for ever; here I will make MY home, for such is MY desire.' Because, in Christian terms '*You are the Temple*', these words can also be heard addressed personally to you and to every aspect of your human nature.

The clearer this truth becomes to you – the more it becomes 'heart knowledge' – the clearer you will see that this Word is for *every* human being, for every last scrap of this and every planet, and for the vastness of space in which they are set: You, everyone and everything is MY Temple, loved, beautiful, glorious, holy, in which to find happiness, blessing, a humble awareness of ME, and all the rest.

This reminds me of the visionary language of Meister Eckhart:

> You must understand that all creatures are by nature endeavouring to be like God. The heavens would not revolve unles they followed on the track of God or of his likeness. If God were not in all things, nature would stop dead, not working and not wanting, for whether you like it or not, whether you know it or not, nature fundamentally is seeking . . . and tending towards God . . . Nature . . . seeks and ever more hotly . . . pursues the trail of God.[11]

If you have grasped something of this poetic truth, you are bound to be impelled to do the work of thanksgiving and intercession – to allow God to channel his Word through you – to let yourself be caught up in his burning general and particular desire for the well-being of everyone and everything – to share his joy, praise, even ecstacy over all the lovely, beautiful, glorious, holy Temple building that is going on in people and in the whole creation. Channel the Word to all of this. Share the spirit and life of the Word. Saturate all that is good and true. Release the laughter and tears which come with the recognition that the

Word *is* being fulfilled in countless people and places: 'MY resting-place . . . MY home . . . MY desire.'

Here is one delightful example. A couple of years back, my wife and I discovered an excellent prayer card. The words (and the caligraphy) struck us so forcibly that we have since bought and distributed the card by the hundreds:

> I AM THE LORD OF LOVE, I am the one who is moving gently . . . Leading, drawing on into all that is new and good and lovely . . . All that I have for you is good . . . All that you need is available now. Do not rush . . . do not fret . . . do not panic. Just rest and wait . . . and wait and rest. Let the water flow on . . . carrying you. Leave it all to me. For I am the Lord who comes gently to you . . . I am the Lord who loves you deeply. I died . . . I went through Gethsemane for you. How can I lead you into death now? No, I am the Lord of life and I lead you on into new and wonderfully green pastures. There is no need to struggle any more. Just step on gently . . . in my love. I have you by the hand . . . I am not rushing you. We will go together into tomorrow and all the tomorrows . . . I am with you . . . Trust me for I cannot let you go.[12]

A person who can write like that is on the way to becoming a magnificent holy Temple. What a profound joy it is, in the silence, to utter the Word directly to the writer, 'MY resting place . . . MY home . . . MY desire', with something of the sense of accomplished fact rather than remote aspiration.

The example I have given is explicitly Christian. But *anything* creative, anything loving, even the smallest act of human kindness or generosity, is a subject for joyful thanksgiving and intercession.

Share also God's sadness, anger, agony over all that is unlovely, ugly, distorted and evil.[13] The daily newspaper or the television news and documentary broadcasts give plenty of subjects for this aspect of prayer.

Not a day passes without news of the destructive things human beings are doing to themselves, to others, or to our planet and its outer space. A mere glance at my today's *local* newspaper reveals multiple crashes on several major roads, neglected children burned to death in a house fire, the hunts for a rapist and a murderer, the suicide of a solicitor, a housewives' fraud ring. Add to this the national and international bad news, become aware of the appalling irresponsibility, neglect, abuse, brutality, oppression, depression, cheating, stealing, and you will know how much Temple building there is yet to do – how much the world needs to hear, receive and live by the Word which proclaims that 'This is MY resting place for ever; here I will make MY home, for such is MY desire.'

Suppose, during this aspect of prayer, you use your imagination in a disciplined and sensitive manner.[14] Suppose, say, you look realistically, as if through the eyes of God and in the light of the Word of God, at some horrifically tragic or brutal incident – something that makes you sick to your stomach – something that tears you to pieces and breaks your heart. You may be tempted to 'turn off', because you feel you cannot bear it, just as some people turn off the television set when confronted with revolting extremes of starvation, obscenity or violence.

The contemplative way is not to turn off but to stay with it, to be exposed to the *whole* of life, to the good, the bad and the ugly, and to bathe and penetrate it all in the light and power of the Word.

It does not matter whether you feel that, in some cases, the channelling of the Word is a pointless, fruitless waste of time and energy. There is no such thing as a hopeless case. I suggest that the more hopeless a particular case *seems* to be, the more vital it is that the Word you carry within you be 'belched'[15] from you, perhaps even with the violence of a volcanic eruption:

'MY resting-place . . . MY home . . . MY desire' . . .

Lord, I long for the fulfilment of your true Word. I will remember your Word because it is a lamp to light my path. When your Word is revealed all is light. Grant me life according to your Word. Amen.[16]

As you habitually own or embody the Word for your-self – as you learn to pray according to the spirit and life of the Word – as you practise the regular habit of keeping the 'Watchword', you will slowly or quickly but inevitably become a living sign or witness of that Word. If you are able to carry around with you the gut conviction that you are the Temple, the desired resting place and home of God, the human things you are and do will be 'full of grace and truth'. The Temple language of the Psalms will also take on new meaning for you: 'O Lord, I love the beauty of thy House, the place where thy glory dwells . . . Holiness is the beauty of thy Temple . . . The praise thy name deserves, O God, is heard at earth's farthest bounds.' Such words are both humbling and exalting.

'MY resting-place . . . MY home . . . MY desire.'

MY Name shall be there

MY Name shall be there.

(1 KINGS 8.29)

Throughout the Bible the word 'name', either refer-
ring to God or spoken by God, occurs hundreds of
times.[1]

As we have seen, King Solomon built a splendid
Temple with a magnificent inner sanctuary. Before the
building work had even begun, Solomon had stated
his prime reason for building a Temple: 'I propose to
build a House in honour of the Name of the Lord my
God.'[2]

When the building of the Temple had been completed, Solomon held a seven-day celebratory festival.
It included a service of blessing and dedication, part
of which consisted of a long and powerful prayer.[3]
Here is an extract in which Solomon prays specifically
about the Temple:

> Solomon, standing in front of the altar of the Lord . . .
> spread out his hands and said, 'O Lord God . . . listen to
> the cry and the prayer which thy servant utters this day,
> that thine eyes may ever be upon this House night and
> day, this place of which thou didst say, "MY Name shall be
> there."'

In the same prayer, Solomon prays that 'all peoples
of the earth may . . . learn that this House . . . bears
thy Name.' Later, God is represented as replying to
Solomon's prayer:

> 'I have heard the prayer which you have offered ME; I have
> consecrated this House which you have built, to receive

MY Name for all time, and MY eyes and MY heart shall be fixed on it for ever . . . This House . . . which I chose . . . shall receive MY Name for all time.'[4]

As might be expected, the Psalms are rich in references to the Name of God and to the power and impact of that Name. God is a shelter to those who love his Name. His Name is glorious, provoking glory, praise and blessing with song, dance and instruments. His Name is a tower of strength and source of help from the sanctuary. For the sake of his Name a person is guided along the right path. For the honour of his Name sin and wickedness, however great, is forgiven and wiped out. His Name inspires trust and gladness and has power to save. Hands are lifted up in prayer in his Name. The story of God's deeds brings his Name very near. All nations shall honour and bow down before his Name. His Name binds people together in unity of heart. Through his Name heads may be held high. His Name inspires awe. By his Name people are blessed. His Name is high above all others.[5]

Such images are scattered freely through many other Old Testament writings. Isaiah claims that the Name of God is 'heart's desire' – a Name to be known – a holy Name.[6] Jeremiah announces that the Name to be given to God is 'The Lord our Righteousness'.[7] Typically, Lamentations speaks of calling on the Name 'from the depths of the pit.'[8] Ezekiel represents God as saying, 'I will hallow MY great Name . . . MY holy Name I will make known in the midst of MY people . . . I will be jealous for MY holy Name . . . Do you see the place of MY throne, the place where I set MY feet, where I will dwell for ever?'[9] Micah refers to 'The majesty of the Name'.[10]

Clearly, in the Old Testament, the Name of God is of central importance and significance. The Name of God is a way of identifying the character and work of God

himself.[11] God is 'jealous' for his Name in the sense
that he wants to keep, protect, enhance and promote
his good reputation, his fame and renown. When
prophets and others speak of acting 'in the Name' of
God, they mean according to the nature and character
– the mind, heart and will – of God himself. It carries
with it the sense of being commissioned to speak or act
on God's behalf.

The main theme of this book is that '*You* are the
Temple.' The food for silent contemplation is five
simple, direct but far-reaching words of God: 'MY
Name shall be there' – there written into your human
nature – there at the core of your being, in that inner
sanctuary. 'This is MY desire and longing for you,' God
seems to be saying:

Bear in your body the marks of MY character and work.
Keep, protect, enhance and promote MY good Name – MY
reputation, fame and renown. I have chosen you and
commissioned you to think, feel and act according to MY
character. Build a Temple in honour of MY glorious, holy,
majestic, awe-inspiring Name. Let everyone know that
you bear MY Name. Let those who love MY Name find in
you a home, shelter, tower of strength, help and guidance, forgiveness, saving power and blessing, especially
when they cry out from the depths of agony and despair.
Let them see in you a House of Prayer. Let them hear in
you the story of MY wonderful deeds – deeds that have
made MY Name memorable. By the marks of MY character
and presence in you, bind people together in unity of
heart. Encourage them to hold their heads high because
MY Name is high above all others.

I have chosen and consecrated you to receive MY Name
for all time, and MY eyes and MY heart will be fixed on you
for ever. I will hallow MY great Name. MY holy Name I will
make known in the midst of MY people. See in yourself the
place of MY throne, the place where I set MY feet, where I
will dwell for ever. MY Name shall be there – there in every

fibre of your humanity. MY Name shall be there. But remember always that I will be jealous for MY holy Name.

Why is God jealous? Because, as was the case with many of the priests and people of Jerusalem, you can let God down and give him a bad Name. The psalmist cries out to God: 'They set fire to thy sanctuary, tore down and polluted the shrine sacred to thy Name.'[12] As we saw in the previous chapter, God can blaze with loving anger at those who neglect, defile, misuse or abuse the Temple, simply because such behaviour 'profanes'[13] the Name of God and, as part of the Ten Commandments express it: 'I, the Lord your God, AM a jealous God . . . You shall not make wrong use of the Name of the Lord your God; the Lord will not leave unpunished the man who misuses his Name.'[14] Let Jeremiah's devastating clarity about false religion and its consequences reflect a major concern of many of the Old Testament prophets. Jeremiah hears God speaking of appalling neglect, deceit and exploitation – God who then says, 'You come and stand before ME in this House, which bears MY Name, and say, "We are safe"; safe, you think, to indulge in all these abominations. Do you think that this House, this House which bears MY Name, is a robbers' cave?'[15]

The work of being and becoming a Temple built to the honour of God's holy Name, carries with it far-reaching moral implications. If you are taking the work of Temple building, or contemplation, seriously, the things you think and feel, the things you think and feel *about*, and the things you do, are to honour and reflect the good Name of God – to radiate his glory, holiness, majesty and splendour.

To borrow some words once uttered by King David: 'Devote yourselves therefore, heart and soul, to seeking the guidance of the Lord your God, and set about building his sanctuary . . . a House built in honour of his Name.'[16]

'You are the Temple' and 'MY Name shall be there.'

The way to 'set about' it is by the discipline of contemplative prayer and life, and by making 'the fullest possible use of all (other) means of becoming holy which God freely gives us.'[17]

Much earlier in this book (p. 15), I spoke of *Jesus* as the perfect Temple. He lived and died only to glorify the holy Name of the Father. He lived out the prayer he taught his disciples to say: 'Our Father in heaven, thy Name be hallowed.'[18] The Gospel according to John represents Jesus as saying, 'MY deeds done in MY Father's Name are MY credentials.' In the Garden of Gethsemane, Jesus cried out, 'Father, glorify thy Name.' The voice of God replied, 'I have glorified it, and I will glorify it again.' Before Jesus's arrest, he prayed long and hard for his disciples. In that prayer he twice referred to his Father's Name: 'I have made thy Name known'; 'Holy Father, protect by the power of thy Name those whom thou hast given ME.'[19]

But throughout the New Testament something new comes to light. The word 'name' is used both of God *and* of Jesus the Christ. In Christian experience and teaching, the Name, person and work of God cannot be separated from the Name, person and work of Christ. They are identical. So we find Jesus represented as saying such things as 'Where two or three have met together in MY Name, I AM there among them.' 'Anything you ask in MY Name I will do, so that the Father may be glorified in the Son. If you ask anything in MY Name I will do it.' 'In very truth I tell you, if you ask the Father for anything in MY Name, he will give it you.'[20]

The Gospel according to John claims that everything it records has been 'in order that you may hold the faith that Jesus is the Christ, the Son of God, and that through this faith you may possess life by his Name.'[21]

This theme is expounded to great effect in Acts of the Apostles and in many of the New Testament Letters. Christians are encouraged, 'Whatever you are doing, whether you speak or act, do everything in the Name of the Lord Jesus.'[22] The Letter of Paul to the Philippians proclaims in fine and familiar language, that

> God raised [Christ Jesus] to the heights and bestowed on him the Name above all Names, that at the Name of Jesus every knee should bow – in heaven, on earth, and in the depths – and every tongue confess, 'Jesus Christ is Lord', to the glory of God the Father.[23]

Finally, The Revelation of John[24] presents a vision of the risen, exalted, majestic, cosmic Christ:

> His eyes flamed like fire, and on his head were many diadems. Written upon him was a Name known to none but himself, and . . . he was called the Word of God . . . And on his robe and on his thigh there was written the Name: 'King of kings and Lord of lords.'[25]

It is *that* Christ, Christ *the* living Word of God, the Christ whose Name is 'like perfume poured out',[26] who can be heard speaking the eternal and prophetic words – words to be received 'in silent awe and adoration'[27] – words to be made incarnate in *your* flesh:

'MY Name . . . there.'

(*Silence*)

Now turn your attention to the demanding work of responding to this Word, in prayer and action, especially the work of intercession – of being a vehicle, instrument, channel of this particular Word, for other people, the world and all that exists: 'MY Name shall be there.' Every human being and the whole universe is to become a holy Temple to the honour and glory of the Lord's holy Name. Be disciplined about this intercessory work. At this stage you may find it helpful to re-read the intercessory parts of the previous chapters (pp. 6–9, 16–19, 27–30, 37–41).

Silent intercessory prayer, as I have indicated earlier, can be a joyful or sorrowful experience.

Suppose, for example, you are looking at Mother Teresa of Calcutta. It might be said with considerable truth, that she is a living, breathing, flesh and blood Temple of the living God – that the holy Name of God and of his Christ is *there*, for all to see.

Someone once wrote of Mother Teresa:

> For those of us who find difficulty in grasping with our minds Christ's great propositions of love which make such dedication possible, someone like Mother Teresa is a godsend. She is this love in person; through her, we can reach it, and hold it, and incorporate it in ourselves. Everyone feels this. I was watching recently the faces of people as they listened to her – just ordinary people who had crowded into a school hall to hear her. Every face, young and old, simple and sophisticated, was rapt, hanging on her words; not because of the words themselves – they were ordinary enough – but because of her. Some quality that came across over and above the words held their attention. A luminosity seemed to fill the school hall, illumining the rapt faces, penetrating every mind and heart.[28]

It is only a little over ten years ago, that Mother Teresa 'came to a new awareness that deep contemplation leads to evangelization',[29] that as recently as 1977, she founded a male branch of contemplatives known as 'Brothers of the Word' whose basic 'rule' is:

Know the Word of God
Love the Word of God
Live the Word of God
Give the Word of God
And the Word of God will make you holy.[30]

To be true Brothers of the Word, states the expanded
'rule',

> we must also be true Brothers of the Silence: God spoke
> only one Word and he spoke it in an eternal silence. We
> must hide within it if we want to understand it: this Word
> is his Son Jesus Christ.[31]

What a joy it can be, armed perhaps with the photographs in *Something Beautiful for God*, simply, imaginat-
ively and silently to share the living and active Word
which the Lord has given: 'MY Name . . . there' – there
in every part of Teresa's being, in everyone who
shares her vision and work.[32]

By stark and painful contrast, a newspaper reports
the arrest of a husband and wife. The wife had held a
young girl down while the husband repeatedly raped
her. Three people involved in a savage and tragic
event. Both perpetrators and victim are called to precisely the same destiny as Mother Teresa and her
co-workers. The husband and wife stand accused of
defiling and abusing both their own and their victim's
Temple. The Word is for each and all of them: 'MY
Name . . . there!' If the Word is truly working in us, it
will breed a strong sense of compassion,[33] especially
towards the victim. Knowing the kind of scars her
experience will leave, knowing that she will probably
have to face a long and difficult process of healing, we
may well find ourselves drawing upon and channelling other Words of God that are beginning to make
their home in us: 'Come to ME . . . and find rest.' 'You

are MY resting place . . . MY home . . . MY desire.' 'MY Name shall be there.' 'MY Name . . . there.'

'MY Name . . . there' . . .

Lord, I praise you, bless and adore you for your Word. Enable me, all humankind and all creation, to build a Temple entirely to the honour of your holy Name. Let it be to me according to your Word and Will. Amen.[34]

'If a man love ME,' said Jesus, 'he will keep MY Word.'[35] Keep the Watchword he has given you. Keep it with you and never lose sight of it. Care for it. Guard it with your life. Use it. Recall it before you sleep, when you wake, and throughout each day.

Assume, for a moment, that you *are* keeping the Word – that you *are* embodying the spirit and life of the Word – that the Word *is* the solid rock on which your prayer and life is built[36] – that the Word *is* governing and colouring your attitude and behaviour to yourself, and your approach to people and events.

If that is, in any sense, a true assumption, you will be able authentically to utter something of King Solomon's prayer:

Heaven itself, the highest heaven cannot contain thee, how much less this House that I have built! Yet attend to the prayer and the supplication of thy servant, O Lord my God, listen to the cry and the prayer which thy servant utters this day, that thine eyes may ever be upon this House night and day, this place of which thou didst say, 'MY Name shall be there'.[37]

Such words are both humbling and exalting!

'MY Name shall be there.'

I will be an inner spring

I . . . will be an inner spring always welling up for eternal life.

(JOHN 4.14)

In ordinary conversation, the word 'spring' usually means 'source of water', that is, a natural spring. In general terms, water has enormous power: it can be devastatingly destructive as well as an essential source and sustainer of all life. The land of Palestine has always been short of water. Its availability cannot be guaranteed for people, animals, or plants. This is the reason why water, or the absence of water, came to have such prominence in the Scriptures, and also why water came to have great symbolic meaning.

For the Hebrew, the word 'water' included cloud, mist, rain, or dew; spring, stream, canal, pond, lake, or cistern; or simply drinking water. In a *literal* sense, all these things were vital – vital as a source of drinking water for people, sheep, goats, cattle, and for watering crops – vital for washing body and clothing. The prophetic vision of the future included an abundant supply of fresh, clean, cool water.

The use of water as a symbol or image, especially as a way of understanding the relationship between God and his people, was very much derived from the physical experience of both the destructive and life-giving power of water.[1]

Firstly, water can be *destructive*. Overflowing rivers and streams, and heavy rainfall, threaten and flood dry land. The Scriptures use the ancient story of Noah and the Flood[2] to symbolize both God's judgement on

53

sinners and the salvation of the righteous few who escape that judgement. The Flood water not only destroyed ungodly people, it also buoyed up those who were in Noah's ark. As the first letter of Peter puts it: 'They . . . refused obedience long ago, while God waited patiently in the days of Noah and the building of the ark, and in the ark a few persons, eight in all, were brought to safety through the water.'[3]

God's judgement and salvation became essential elements throughout both Old and New Testaments. For example, the water that drowned every last man of Pharaoh's pursuing army was the same water that had moved back to allow the Israelites to go through on dry ground.[4] Israel's leaders and prophets looked back appreciatively to this event. They saw it as a symbol or sign of God's special relationship with his Chosen People. Overwhelming waters of destruction and judgement fall on the enemies of God's people.[5]

God's people cannot, however, assume that they are necessarily safe from destruction. If they fail to *be* God's people, the waters of destruction and judgement, in the form of, say, an Assyrian invasion, could well fall upon them.[6] Yet even then, God would re-member *the* Flood and his promise to Noah:

> In sudden anger
> I hid MY face from you for a moment;
> but now have I pitied you with a love which never fails . . .
> These days recall for ME the days of Noah:
> as I swore that the waters of Noah's flood
> should never again pour over the earth,
> so now I swear to you
> never again to be angry with you or reproach you.
> Though the mountains move and the hills shake,
> MY love shall be immovable and never fail.[7]

Flood water as a symbol of trouble is often expressed in the Psalms. The psalmist complains that he finds

himself up to his neck in deep water.[8] This kind of
symbolic use of water may link directly with the
baptism of Jesus and with Christian baptism generally. The Gospel according to Luke represents Jesus as
saying, 'I have a baptism to undergo.'[9] He 'may have
meant, I must be submerged, overwhelmed, sunk in
the waters of affliction. He saw his rejection by the
Jews, and his death, as an overwhelming of himself.'[10]

Jesus is also represented as saying, 'Can you . . . be
baptised with the baptism I AM baptised with?'[11]
Christian baptism is a way of identifying *ourselves* with
the suffering and death of Jesus:

> He says to [us], Let suffering overwhelm you, allow
> yourself to be plunged into it, to be baptised by it. Don't
> run away from it, or evade it – suffer it. Let it run over you
> like a flood of water . . . The disciples of Jesus still have his
> baptism . . . in two ways. First . . . in the Sacrament of
> baptism . . . [and secondly] . . . in the events of [our]
> daily life . . . [the] disasters, afflictions, causes of suffer-
> ing, which come to everybody in the course of daily life.[12]

St Teresa of Avila cannot 'find anything more
appropriate to explain some spiritual experiences than
water'.[13] She also describes the highest state of prayer
as a saturating downpour of heavy rain, so overwhelming that it leads to fainting, swooning, loss of
breath and bodily strength. St Teresa questions what
this experience means. The Lord says to her, '[The
soul] dies to itself wholly . . . in order that it may fix
itself more and more on ME; it is no longer itself that
lives, but I.'[14]

This book is about embodying the Christ Word –
about allowing yourself to be totally plunged into or
saturated by the Word – about accumulating a vast
inner reservoir which issues and bubbles up for the
work of creative prayer and life. When Jesus says 'I *will*'
– 'I will be an inner spring, always welling up for

eternal life', he means that he wants, desires, aches, longs to be an inner spring in you. The contemplative way is about being flooded, deluged, soaked by the Word so that it and he can become an inner spring.

Secondly, water has a *cleansing* power. In the Bible, water for ritual cleansing is of supreme importance. Whenever possible 'living water' (which means 'running water') was to be used. Inside Solomon's Temple, there was a huge, round, cast metal container holding 'two thousand bath[15] of water.' There were also five large wheeled trolleys down each side of the Temple, each carrying a bronze basin 'each holding forty bath.'[16] This vast quantity of water, about fourteen and a half thousand gallons, stood as a reminder of the Levitical rules for ritual cleansing.[17]

The prophetic tradition however, warned that ritual cleansing was not enough. What was needed was an *inner* cleansing – the removal of everything that defiles and corrupts individuals and nations.

Inevitably, the poetry of the Psalms picks up this theme:

> Be gracious to me, O God, in thy true love;
> in the fullness of thy mercy blot out my misdeeds.
> Wash away all my guilt
>   and cleanse me from my sin . . .
> Sprinkle me, that I may be clean;
> wash me, that I may be whiter than snow . . .
> Create a pure heart in me, O God.[18]

The prophet Ezekiel pursues this theme of inner cleanliness. Through Ezekiel, God says to his people:

> I will sprinkle clean water over you, and you shall be clean from all that defiles you; I will cleanse you from the taint of all your idols. I will give you a new heart and put a new spirit within you.[19]

56

For Ezekiel, the cleansing spring had its source in a rebuilt Temple:

> [A man] brought me . . . to the gate of the Temple, and I saw a spring of water issuing from under the terrace of the Temple . . . The water was running down along the right side, to the south of the altar. He took me out through the northern gate and brought me round by an outside path to the eastern gate of the court, and water was trickling from the right side. When the man went out eastwards he had a line in his hand. He measured a thousand cubits and made me walk through the water; it came up to my ankles. He measured another thousand and made me walk through the water; it came up to my knees. He measured another thousand and made me walk through the water; it was up to my waist. Another thousand, and it was a torrent I could not cross, for the water had risen and was now deep enough to swim in . . . 'Mark this, man', he said, and led me back to the bank of the torrent. When we came back to the bank I saw a great number of trees on each side. He said to me, 'This water flows out . . . [and] will reach that sea whose waters are foul, and they will be sweetened. When any one of the living creatures that swarm upon the earth comes where the torrent flows, it shall draw life from it. The fish shall be innumerable; for these waters come here so that the others may be sweetened, and where the torrent flows everything shall live . . . Beside the torrent on either bank all trees good for food shall spring up. Their leaves shall not wither, their fruit shall not cease . . . For their water comes from the sanctuary.'[20]

Symbolically, the spring of water from the Temple sanctuary is none other than God himself who *is* the 'spring of living water.'[21]

'*You* are the Temple.' Can you begin to sense in yourself, that 'inner spring' of God and of Christ the Word, issuing from your inner sanctuary? A spring which becomes, not only a trickle with which people can splash themselves, but a great, deep torrent in which they can swim and from which all humankind and all creation can draw life? 'Where the torrent flows everything shall live.' Are you aware that your inner reservoir, and the spring, stream, surging river that comes from it is utterly clean, clear, pure and sweet – that it is meeting and sweetening the 'foul waters' in you and in the world around you?

Of the four Gospel writings, only John explores the theme of Christ as 'living water'. In his conversation with the woman at the well,[22] Jesus is represented as saying to her, 'The water that I shall give . . . will be an inner spring . . .'

The New Testament in general, links the Old Testament vision of cleansing and purifying water, with the baptism of Jesus and of Christians.[23] The Gospel according to John links living water with the Holy Spirit.[24] The Letter of Paul to the Ephesians connects living water with the Word.[25] The Letter to the Hebrews, which has much to say about the significance of the Temple, speaks of 'guilty hearts sprinkled clean . . . , bodies washed with pure water.'[26] The Letter of Paul to Titus asserts that God 'saved us through the water of rebirth and the renewing power of the Holy Spirit. For he sent down the Spirit upon us plentifully.'[27]

With such a background, it is no surprise to find that the Church's contemplative tradition speaks of the experience of being cleansed and purified by the life-giving Word and Spirit of God and especially of his Christ.[28] It has often been linked, for example, with the first of the so-called 'Three Ways' or stages of growth in prayer and creative living, known technically as the 'Purgative Way' or, to use the Greek word, 'catharsis'.[29]

Images of purification other than water, are used to

great effect within the contemplative tradition: for example, becoming innocent like an infant child; the fire of love which burns away impurities; a movement away from multiplicity, complexity and total chaos, towards singleness, simplicity and stillness; resistance to temptation; the 'dark night' experience; the practice of virtue and obedience.

The Bible itself uses purging or cleansing images other than water. One that relates directly to the theme of this book is the metaphor of a 'pruning knife', used for cutting back, or cleaning, fruiting vines, trees and bushes – a pruning knife which is nothing less than the Word of Christ himself: 'You are *already* made clean [or pruned] by the Word that I spoke to you.'[30]

Jesus longs to be an 'inner spring' in you – to be a cleansing, purifying, purging, cathartic Word and Spirit, in you, for you, and through you.

Thirdly, the symbol of *drinking* water – water to quench thirst. The Psalmist, the prophets and the New Testament writers frequently and poetically recall Israel's desert experience:[31]

> [God] cleft the rock in the wilderness
> and gave them water to drink, abundant as the sea;
> he brought streams out of the cliff
> and made water run down like rivers.
>
> Dance . . . at the presence of the Lord . . .
> who turned the rock into a pool of water,
>   the granite cliff into a fountain.[32]

The prophet Isaiah in particular, hears God speaking of water for the thirsty, in both a physical and a figurative sense:

> The wretched and the poor look for water and find none,
>   their tongues are parched with thirst;

59

but I the Lord will . . . open rivers among the
sand-dunes
  and wells in the valleys.

I will provide water in the wilderness
  and rivers in the barren desert,
    where MY chosen people may drink.[33]

And figuratively:

I will pour out MY spirit . . . and MY blessing . . .

Come all who are thirsty, come, fetch water . . .
Come to ME and listen to MY words,
  hear ME, and you shall have life.[34]

The ever popular Shepherd Psalm is a constant reminder that throughout history, God has been
shepherd to his chosen flock and has always enabled
his people to find water for their thirst.[35]

Again, the New Testament inevitably takes up the
theme and proclaims that Christ himself *is* the rock
from which the living, thirst-quenching water pours.[36]
The Christ who both is and gives the living water, says
of himself:

Whoever drinks the water that I shall give . . . will never
suffer thirst any more. The water that I shall give . . . will
be an inner spring always welling up for eternal life.

Whoever believes in ME shall never be thirsty.

If anyone is thirsty let him come to ME; whoever believes
in ME, let him drink. As Scripture says, 'Streams of living
water shall flow out from within him.'[37]

Finally, the Revelation of John sees and hears a regal,
heavenly Christ who announces,

A draught from the water-springs of life will be MY free gift
to the thirsty.

Come forward, you who are thirsty; accept the water of
life, a free gift to all who desire it.[38]

We have by no means exhausted the image of water as a sign of the relationship between God and his people.[39] Both the Bible and the contemplative tradition are abundantly, inexhaustibly rich in water images: to symbolize God and his Christ as judge and saviour; to symbolize the power of his Word and Spirit to cleanse and purify, and to quench the thirst of those who are spiritually parched.

The contemplative tradition would agree that the psalmist gives perfect expression to the last of these:

> As a hind longs for the running streams,
> so do I long for thee, O God.
> With my whole being I thirst for God, the living God.
>
> O God, thou art my God, I seek thee early
>   with a heart that thirsts for thee . . .
> like a dry and thirsty land that has no water.
>   So longing, I come before thee in the sanctuary.[40]

The contemplative discipline of silently 'drinking in' the Word – the judging, saving, purging, refreshing Word – enables the Word to become an inner reservoir upon which to draw for all circumstances of living. That inner reservoir is nothing less than the indwelling Christ himself – the Christ who issues from the inner sanctuary of the Temple which you yourself are – the Christ who is always bubbling up for LIFE! – the Christ who says,

> 'I . . . will be an inner spring.'

(Silence)

Turn again to the work of being a channel of the Word. 'Channel', in the context of this chapter, is particularly appropriate. A channel is primarily connected with running (or 'living') water along, say, the bed of a river or canal. The Word and Spirit of God which you are slowly or quickly receiving and embodying, is itself 'living water' – Word and Spirit for channelling to individuals or groups, towns, cities, nations, the world and all creation – a world and creation under judgement, ripe for the saving, cleansing, refreshing, restoring power of the living Word and life-giving Spirit.

As you do this work of intercession or channelling, you *may* experience a sense, even a profound sense, that the 'living water' is tangibly bubbling up and flowing from your inner sanctuary – from the very middle of your being, from your open hands,[41] or even from eyes flooded with tears of joy or sorrow.[42] You *may* begin to understand, as a matter of experience, something of what God meant when he spoke to St Catherine of Siena. God spoke to her of a stage

> of souls who have attained perfection in loving their neighbours and love ME without any self-interest. These weep and their weeping is perfect . . . I want you to know that all tears come from the heart.[43]

Whatever pattern you use for intercessory work – whatever effect it may or may not have on you – however much or little you share God's loving desire for the well-being of all his people and all creation, as long as you channel the Word and the Spirit of that Word, it *will* be doing the work God sent it to do:

> As the rain and the snow come down from heaven
> and do not return until they have watered the earth,
>   making it blossom and bear fruit . . .
> so shall the Word which comes from MY mouth prevail;
>   it shall not return to ME fruitless
> without accomplishing MY purpose
>   or succeeding in the task I gave it.[44]

To sum it all up with Louis Evely's utter simplicity: contemplative prayer 'is opening ourselves to God so that he can open us to others.'[45]

'I . . . will be an inner spring.' . . .

Lord, I praise, bless and adore you for your judging, saving, cleansing, life-giving Word; and I offer and present to you, as far as I am able, all that I am, all that I have, and all that I do, as an emptiness to be filled by you and by your Word, until you are all in all, and I am complete; through him who is the embodiment of your Word, Jesus Christ. Amen.

An encouragement to keep the Watchword. Keep it, not only as a constant reminder of the Lord's presence and Word for you, but also of the way you are called to be, if you are to be true to the God in whose image you are made.

In your daily attitude and behaviour; in the way you look at people, speak to them and touch them; in the way you look at and relate to the world and all creation, let everyone and everything see in you a Temple from which flows the fountain of life – a Temple from which justice and righteousness issue like an ever-flowing stream; a Temple by which deserts of every kind are changed into pools, and dried-up people into springs of living water; a Temple living a good and truthful life; a Temple from which love flows; a Temple from which the voice of God sounds like a mighty torrent; a Temple enabling the whole earth to be filled with the knowledge and glory of God, as the waters cover the sea.[46]

If, in any sense, you are truly co-operating, in both prayer and action, with the Word and will of God, then, as he himself went on to say:

You shall indeed go out with joy
and be led forth in peace.

Before you mountains and hills shall break into cries of jo
and all the trees of the wild shall clap their hands . . .
   all this shall win[ME] a great Name,
     imperishable, a sign for all time.[47]

I want to let John Ruusbroec speak a concluding
word for me:

A person who has been sent [from contemplation] into the
world is full of truth and rich in all virtues. He seeks
nothing of his own but only the glory of the One who sent
him. He is accordingly righteous and truthful in all things
and has a rich and generous foundation which rests on
God's own richness. He will therefore always flow forth to
all who need him, for the living spring of the Holy Spirit is
so rich that it can never be drained dry. Such a person is a
living and willing instrument of God with which God
accomplishes what he wishes in the way he wishes . .
May God grant that we all attain this. Amen.[48]

AMEN!

       'I . . . will be an inner spring.'

APPENDIX: FURTHER WORDS FOR CONTEMPLATION

If you have been able to work patiently and carefully through this book, it will have taken you six months to have heard and received, with all the love the Lord has so far given you, the following Words of God:

> Come to ME, all who labour and are heavy laden, and I will give you rest. Take MY yoke upon you and learn from ME; for I AM gentle and lowly in heart, and you will find rest for your soul. For MY yoke is easy, and MY burden is light.

> Consider your way of life.

> Build a Temple acceptable to ME, where I can show MY glory.

> [You are] MY resting-place for ever; [in you] I will make MY home, for such is MY desire.

> MY Name shall be there.

> I . . . will be an inner spring, always welling up for eternal life.

If you were to spend the rest of your life contemplating *only* these living Words, they would never lose their significance, freshness or cutting edge. There is rich food and drink here to last a lifetime and more than a lifetime.

They nevertheless represent only a tiny fraction of the inexhaustible riches of the Hebrew/Christian Scriptures – words and phrases which 'come from the mouth of God',[1] and which are all for his glory and for your good and the good of all humanity and all creation.

For what it may be worth, I list those Words or Sayings of God which have received no more than a passing mention in my book, together with a few others that come to mind because they link, in some sense, with my main theme. Each Word is, so to speak, at least a month's supply!

'I will fill this Temple with glory.'
'I AM with you . . . . Take heart!'
'Begin the work, for I AM with you.'
'MY Spirit is present [within] you.'
Haggai

'I will give joy in MY House of prayer.'
'MY House shall be called a House of prayer.'
Isaiah and Matthew

'Make your home in ME, as I make MINE in you.'
John

'I have consecrated this [Temple] which you have built.'
'MY eyes and MY heart will be fixed on [you] for ever.'
1 Kings

'I will hallow MY great Name.'
'I will make known MY holy Name.'
Ezekiel

'Anything you ask in MY Name I will do.'
John

(Please note that on the theme of the 'Name' of God, each one of the many 'I AM' Sayings are of incalculable value for contemplation, e.g.: 'I AM WHO I AM.' 'I AM full of compassion . . . of strength, justice and power.' 'I AM filled with tenderness.' 'I AM holy.' 'I AM gentle and lowly in heart.' 'I AM the Good Shepherd . . . the Light of the world . . . the Bread of life.' 'I AM the Door.' 'I AM the Word.' and many more!)

'I have pitied you with a love that never fails.'
'MY love shall be immovable and never fail.'
Isaiah

'Can you be baptised with MY baptism?'
Mark

'I will sprinkle clean water over you.'
'You shall be clean from all that defiles you.'
'I will cleanse you from . . . all idols.'
'I will give you a new heart.'
'I will . . . put a new spirit within you.'
Ezekiel

'You are . . . made clean by the Word.'
John

'I will pour out MY spirit . . . and MY blessing.'
'Come to ME and listen to MY words . . . and you shall have life.'
Isaiah

'Come forward, you who are thirsty.'
'Accept the water of life, a free gift.'
Revelation

'You shall go out with joy.'
'You shall . . . be led forth in peace.'
'When you pass through deep waters, I AM with you.'
'You will be like a well-watered garden.'
'You will be like a . . . spring whose waters never fail.'
'You shall draw water with joy from the springs of deliverance.'
'I will send peace flowing like a river.'
Isaiah

Even all these are a mere fraction of what a friend once called the Bible's 'inexhaustibly rich abundance of divine vocabulary'.[2] Yet, paradoxically, in contemplation all the rich verbal and visual imagery of the Hebrew/Christian tradition ultimately becomes empty, meaningless and useless. Contemplation is loving God and letting God love us; and love, at its best, becomes lost for words – speechless![3]

NOTES

Scripture references are normally to the New English Bible, unless otherwise indicated. (GNB = Good News Bible; JB = Jerusalem Bible; NIV = New International Version; RSV = Revised Standard Version.)

Preface

1. Hebrews 4.12.
2. Ezekiel 36.26.
3. Acts 17.28.
4. Peter Dodson, *Contemplating the Word* (SPCK 1987).
5. Part of this is reproduced below – Month One, note 4.
6. *Contemplating the Word*, pp. 47–50: 'Distractions [voluntary or otherwise] will always plague our attempts to pay attention to God and his Word . . . The action to take is not to prolong distractions but to get back to the job in hand – deliberately to refocus attention on the Word . . . Distractions are not necessarily destructive. They can be used positively and creatively, to help us to be more disciplined in the quality of our attention to God.'
7. See also Robert Coulson, *On Course in Contemplation* (Fellowship of Contemplative Prayer) pp. 47–50 from which I extract the following: 'Each [contemplative prayer group or retreat session] consists of three periods of about twenty minutes. Each period consists of *up to* [my italics] ten minutes introductory talk, followed by about ten minutes silence. In the last silence the talk and silence may be more closely interwoven, as shown below . . .

   '*The first talk* aims at preparing the *mind* to receive the Words, and best consists of a theological exposition of the Words (theory). Then comes the first silence. This opens with a two minutes response to the "comfortable words". "Come to ME, all whose work is hard, whose load is heavy, and I will give you rest." Then a minute or two for self-examination and renunciation of any burden of sinfulness. Then the silence, mentally repeating the Word [chosen for contemplation].

'*The second talk* aims to prepare the *heart* to receive the Words, and best consists of up to ten minutes account of how the [group or retreat leader] has experienced the significance of the Words himself (theory proved by experience). The second silence then follows, in which all . . . mentally repeat . . . the Words.

'*The third talk* aims to prepare the *will* to receive the Words, and to let them "work", moving the will accordingly (theory put into practice). This best consists of a few minutes practice in applying the Words to some personal difficulty, and then . . . intercession . . .

'The hour's session ends with a brief thanksgiving and self-offering.'

8. Deuteronomy 8.3; Matthew 4.4.
9. Psalm 29.4 GNB.
10. As quoted in R. H. Reinhold (ed.), *Spear of Gold – Revelations of the Mystics* (Burns & Oates 1947), p. 279.

Month One: Come to ME and rest

1. Ecclesiasticus 51.23–7 NEB.
2. J. D. Douglas (ed.), *The New Bible Dictionary* (Inter-Varsity Press 1962), p. 795.
3. John C. Fenton, *Saint Matthew* (Pelican 1963), p. 187.
4. Cf. *Contemplating the Word*, pp. 40–43, of which the following is an extract: 'We should sit in such a way that we are not unnecessarily distracted by our bodies. Our clothing and footwear should be loose and comfortable. Some people prefer not to wear shoes at all.

'Whether we decide to use a chair, meditation stool or carpeted floor, sit straight but never stiffly or rigidly. The spine is not like a ramrod: it has a gentle curve. Be aware of that curve, and sit comfortably and relaxed. The head should rest centrally on the spinal column and not be allowed to settle into the shoulders. The feet and knees should be about shoulder-width apart . . .

'Place the hands lightly and loosely on the thighs, with the palms upwards, in an open and receptive attitude. The whole body, once in the kind of position I have described, takes on an attitude of openness . . . rather like a flower opening itself to the sun. It is as if we were saying to God: "Here I am, open and ready to receive whatever you have to say or give to me in the silence" . . .

'A deep-breathing exercise can [also] assist with the process of relaxation and attention . . . Deep breathing increases the supply of oxygen to the brain, thereby helping us to become more alive, awake, alert, attentive; and the breathing rhythm can be used to help us keep hold of the Word in the silence . . .

'This physical aspect of the discipline will not necessarily be achieved easily . . . We may experience a terrible struggle to *be* still, to *be* relaxed, to *be* open, to *be* attentive. There may even be severe physical reasons for this. For example, I always try to be extra sensitive towards anyone who is physically handicapped . . . It may be impossible for such a person to sit in the way I have described. He or she may need, say, extra back or leg support. For some people, breathing can be a terrible trial. All [that can be done] is to . . . work within . . . personal limitations.

'But the fruit of bodily discipline – of a still, relaxed, open and attentive posture – makes every bit of the struggle worth while.'
5. Robert Coulson, *Into God – An Exercise in Contemplation* (John Murray 1956), pp. 58–9.
6. 1 John 1.8 GNB.
7. Cf. Hebrews 4.13.
8. Extract from a letter from Bishop Kallistos of Diokleia 1988. See also Father Lev Gillet (A monk of the Eastern Church), *The Jesus Prayer* (St Vladimir's Seminary Press 1987), p. 72.
9. John Bagley, *Doors of Perception – icons and their spiritual significance* (Mowbray 1987) represents an excellent modern introduction to icons as aids to prayer. I especially appreciate chapter 4 on 'Biblical Language –

Verbal and Visual Imagery'. See also the Calendar Books from the St Paul Book Centre, entitled *Novgorod, School of Moscow, Baptism of the Rus*, etc.

10. Anthony de Mello sj, *Sadhana – A Way to God* (Image Books 1984), p. 78f.

11. Robert Llewelyn, *A Doorway to Silence – The Contemplative Use of the Rosary* (Darton, Longman and Todd 1986), p. 19.

12. Cf. St Augustine of Hippo, *Confessions*, Book One: 'You have made us to be "toward" you, and our heart is restless until it rests in you.'

13. Cf. Luke 8.11f. Cf. also, *Contemplating the Word*, p. 21: 'When Jesus explained the Parable of the Sower, he said: "The seed is the word of God . . . The seed that fell in good soil stands, for those who not only hear the word, but keep it in the heart, and persist until they bear fruit" . . . The best possible soil in which God may sow the seed of his Word is the soil of silence and stillness . . . Seeds can only grow when the soil is still.

'It is the same with human beings. When we can learn to be still . . . the "Word-seed" can find a place to rest, to germinate, put down strong roots, grow, flourish and bear abundant fruit. The contemplative way is about persisting with the discipline, not only of hearing the Word, but of keeping it in the heart and allowing it to grow and become fruitful . . . for the service of God and his world.'

14. Julian of Norwich, *Showings* (Paulist Press and SPCK 'Classics of Western Spirituality' 1978), p. 225.

15. Father Simon Holden cr shared this idea at a conference on prayer.

16. Romans 8.22.

17. Cf. Jeremiah 20.9.

18. This prayer is based on words from the Scriptures: Ezekiel 3.10: 'Listen carefully . . . to all that I have to say to you.' Psalm 119.160: 'Thy word is founded in truth.' John 6.63: 'The words which I have spoken to you are both spirit and life.' Matthew 7.24: 'Anyone who hears these words of MINE and acts upon them is like a wise man who built his house on rock.' It is possible to create

many similar prayers based on what the Scriptures say *about* the Word. Psalm 119 is particularly valuable in this respect. Cf. also Philip Law, *Praying with the New Testament* and *Praying with the Old Testament* (Triangle, 1988 and 1989) for examples of praying the words of Scripture.

19. See *Contemplating the Word*, pp. 74–5: 'A Watchword – a word by which we literally watch ourselves . . . The Watchword represents a constant reminder, not only of the presence and Word of God for you, but also of the way you are to be in the home, at school, in the workplace, at church . . . Above all, the Watchword, whichever one it may be from the Bible's rich store, can become vital food for our *daily* contemplation. The time allocated to this, perhaps once or twice each day, need be no longer than, say, seven minutes. The first two minutes are spent becoming inwardly quiet and still . . . The remaining five minutes are devoted to receiving the Watchword into the mind and heart, ending with a prayer of thanksgiving and dedication. If this kind of daily prayer does, in fact, lead to profound contemplation, the time given to it may naturally be extended to, say, twenty minutes or half an hour.'

20. James 1.22–25 RSV.

Month Two: Consider your life

1. The Jerusalem Bible; Good News Bible; New International Version.
2. Ezra 3.1–3.
3. Ezra 3.8–11.
4. Haggai 1.1–7.
5. 1 Corinthians 3.16; 2 Corinthians 6.19 GNB; John 2.21.
6. Cf. Hebrews 4.12–13; Ephesians 6.17; Revelation 1.16. See also *Contemplating the Word*, pp. 19 and 20.
7. Cf. Emil Brunner, *The Divine Imperative – A Study in Christian Ethics* (Lutterworth 1937), from which I extract the following (p. 118): 'In a Christian ethic we are not dealing with "counsels" nor with exhortations, nor with "values", with something we "prefer" – no, here we are

confronted by a Command which must be taken in dead earnest.'

8. Cf. *Contemplating the Word*, p. 53f: 'The *Old* Testament . . . words must always be subject to a test of authenticity. It could only be a Word for Christians or any other seeker after truth if it can be heard coming, so to speak, from Jesus himself: if it can be heard speaking from the heart of the cross; if it carries the cutting edge of truth; if it reveals a true God and a true humanity. I . . . cannot see any other way of testing the authenticity of the words of God in the Old Testament. Do the words selected for contemplation ring true? Do they ring true to the Christ of the Gospels? Do they speak with incisive clarity from the heart of the cross? . . . Can we hear Christ the Word speaking the prophetic words? If the words do not bear this ring of truth, it is best not to use them.'

9. Roy Campbell, *Poems of St John of the Cross* (Harvill Press 1951), p. 29.

10. Cf. Thomas Merton, *Seeds of Contemplation* (Anthony Clarke 1972), page 12: 'Christ in the parable of the sower long ago told us that "The seed is the word of God." . . . Every expression of the will of God is in some sense a "word" of God and therefore a "seed" of new life.'

11. Cf. Hans Urs von Balthasar, *Prayer* (SPCK 1973), p. 22. In a discussion about contemplation and the Word of God, von Balthasar wrote: 'The word he [Christ] spoke to the weeping Magdalen at the grave is enough: "Mary!" This proper name coming from the mouth of eternal Life is each man's true idea: it is the true I in God, given and uttered to the believer . . . with the compelling might of the love which, of its very nature, demands and appropriates all. Apart from this love, man cannot be understood at all.'

12. Colossians 3.16.

13. Cf. *Contemplating the Word*, p. 55: 'The process of embodying the Word . . . indicates the truth of Jesus's saying: "I will be an inner spring, always welling up for eternal life." (John 4.14) . . . The first-person Word I carry within me is none other than Jesus himself. It is he who says lovingly to me, in me and through me, "I AM",

"I will", "I have", "MY", "ME"; he who speaks the word
of command to "Choose" and "Be" and "Do"; he who
probes with searching questions about where I am, what
I am doing here, and whether I have confidence in his
power to heal.'

14. Jeremiah 8.18, 21; 14.17. Isaiah 16.9.
15. *Alternative Service Book 1980*, copyright © the Central
    Board of Finance of the Church of England, p. 105.
16. Cf. Isaiah 43.10–12; Acts 1.8.
17. See Month One, note 19 (p. 73). Cf. also R. G. Coulson,
    Into God – An Exercise in Contemplation, p. 68f.
18. Deuteronomy 8.3; Matthew 4.4.

Month Three: Build a Temple to MY glory

1. Cf. the *Oxford English Dictionary*.
2. See, for example, *The New Bible Dictionary*, article on the
   'Temple', p. 1242.
3. For a scholarly exploration of the history of this time,
   and Haggai's part in it, I commend Robert H. Pfeiffer,
   Introduction to the Old Testament (Harper, 1948), p. 602f. I
   would however, disagree with his assertion that the
   book Haggai is 'neglible . . . from the point of view of
   . . . religion.' Pfeiffer misses the point when he says that
   Haggai 'is of the greatest importance [only] . . . as a
   historical source' (my italics).
4. Cf. Bernhard W. Anderson, *The Living World of the Old
   Testament*, 3rd edn. (Longman 1978), p. 483.
5. 1 Corinthians 3.16.
6. Cf. *Contemplating the Word*, p. 4f.
7. Ephesians 2.20–22.
8. Julian of Norwich, *Revelations of Divine Love* (Penguin
   1966), p. 81.
9. Psalm 127.1.
10. 1 Kings 7.48–50.
11. Hebrews 4.12 Living Bible.
12. Psalm 12.6.
13. See Geoffrey W. Bromiley, *Theological Dictionary of the
    New Testament* (William B. Eerdmans and Paternoster
    1985), article on the Greek word *akoúō*, p. 34f.
14. Ephesians 5.19.

15. Haggai 1.12.
16. Ezra 3.11–12.
17. Haggai 1.13; 2.4–5.
18. 1 Peter 2.2.
19. From the prayer 'for the whole state of Christ's Church' in the Book of Common Prayer.
20. Ephesians 1.1–4, 9–10, 17–19; 2.20–22; 3.14–19.
21. Cf. *Contemplating the Word*, pp. 71–2.
22. Cf. Psalm 119.105, 160, 34.
23. James 1.21–5 GNB.
24. Jeremiah 7.4–6.
25. 1 Samuel 10.26.
26. James 1.27.

Month Four: MY *resting-place,* MY *home,* MY *desire*

1. *Peake's Commentary on the Bible* (Nelson 1962), p. 441.
2. Psalms 26.8; 93.5; 65.4; 5.7–8; 66.13; 36.8; 84.3–4; 48.9–10.
3. Cf. Song of Songs 8.6–7; Hosea 11.8; Exodus 22.27; Jeremiah 31.20.
4. John 15.3 JB.
5. John Ruusbroec, *The Spiritual Espousals and Other Works* (Paulist Press and SPCK 'Classics of Western Spirituality' 1985), p. 115.
6. E.g. Hosea 6.5: 'Therefore have I lashed you through the prophets and torn you to shreds with MY words.'
7. Malachi 1.2, 2.2f.
8. Psalm 79.1, 69.9.
9. Matthew 21.12–13.
10. Alastair V. Campbell *The Gospel of Anger* (SPCK 1986), pp. 47–8. The Old Testament quotation, is from Jeremiah 6.11 GNB.
11. Quoted in Whitall N. Perry *A Treasury of Traditional Wisdom* (Perennial Books 1971), p. 311.
12. Available from Elizabeth Griffiths, The Gatehouse, All Hallows Convent, Ditchingham, Norfolk.
13. Cf. Jeremiah 4.19: 'Oh, the writhing of MY bowels and the throbbing of MY heart!' Jeremiah 8.18, 21: 'How can I bear MY sorrow? I AM sick at heart . . . I AM wounded at the sight of MY people's wound; I go like a mourner,

overcome with horror.' Isaiah 16.9–11: I will weep . . . I will drench you with MY tears . . . MY heart throbs . . . and MY very soul.'

14. Cf. Thomas Merton, *Contemplation in a World of Action* (Unwin Paperbacks 1980), sections on 'The Imagination' and 'Liberating the Imagination', pp. 343–8.
15. St Augustine of Hippo somewhere speaks powerfully of God belching his Word.
16. Prayer derived from Psalm 119.

Month Five: MY Name shall be there

1. A classical treatment of the subject which relates directly to contemplative experience is Pseudo-Dionysius, *The Divine Names* (Paulist Press and SPCK 'Classics of Western Spirituality' 1987), pp. 47–131. I also commend Sarah Hornby, *At The Name of Jesus*, (Marshall Morgan & Scott 1983).
2. 1 Kings 5.5.
3. 1 Kings 8.22–53.
4. 1 Kings 9.3 and 2 Kings 21.7.
5. Shelter, Psalm 5.11; glorious Name, 8.1; glory, praise and blessing, 7.1; 9.2; 29.2; 48.10; 52.9; 63.4; 72.19; 103.1; 113.1–3; 135.1–3; 145.1–2, 21; song and dance, 96.2; 149.3; tower, 20.1–2; 124.8 (cf. Proverbs 18.10); right path, 23.3; 31.3; forgiven, 25.11; 79.9; power to save, 33.21; 54.1; hands lifted up, 63.4; his Name brought near, 75.1; nations bow down, 86.9; unity of heart, 86.11; head held high, 89.24; awe, 111.9; blessed, 118.26; high above all others, 148.13.
6. Isaiah 26.8; 52.6; 57.15.
7. Jeremiah 23.6.
8. Lamentations 3.55.
9. Ezekiel 36.23; 39.7, 25; 43.7.
10. Micah 5.4.
11. Cf. Paul Tournier *What's in a Name?* (SCM Press 1975), p. 81: 'The name . . . is not only the symbol of the person: it is the person itself. What then, are the characteristics of the person? They are its liberty, its capacity for responsible commitment. And what must we do to contract such a commitment, whether it be a contract of employ-

ment, an insurance policy, a will, publishing a book or
exhibiting a picture? We must sign it with our name . . .
The name signifies the person.'

12. Psalm 74.7.
13. Cf. Leviticus 19.12; 20.3; 21.6; 22.2; 22.32.
14. Exodus 20.7.
15. Jeremiah 7.3–11; cf. Matthew 21.12–13.
16. 1 Chronicles 22.19.
17. From the 'Rule' of the international Fellowship of Contemplative Prayer. Details of this Fellowship may be obtained from The Reverend Martin Tunnicliffe, The Vicarage, Tanworth-in-Arden, Solihull, West Midlands, B94 5EB, or from Mrs Ann Dodson, St Helen's Vicarage, 2A Sycamore Terrace, York YO3 7DN.
18. Matthew 6.9. Intriguingly, an ecumenical French translation of the Bible, boldly translated 'Our Father . . . thy Name be hallowed' as 'Make yourself recognised as God'! (see Paul Tournier *What's in a Name?*, p. 81).
19. John 10.25; 12.28; 17.6, 11.
20. Matthew 18.20; John 14.13–14; 16.23.
21. John 20.31.
22. Colossians 3.17.
23. Philippians 2.9–10.
24. In the Revelation of John 2.17, the exalted Christ is represented as saying, 'To him who is victorious I will give . . . a white stone, and on the stone will be written a new Name.' A classical exploration of this text, concerned directly with the quality and style of contemplative prayer and life, is to be found in John Ruusbroec's *The Sparkling Stone* (Paulist Press and SPCK 'Classics of Western Spirituality' 1985) pp. 153–184.
25. Revelation 19.12f. NEB.
26. Song of Songs 1.3. Cf. St Bernard of Clairvaux, *On Loving God* (SCM Press 1959), Sermon Fifteen, pp. 79–88.
27. Two Listeners, *A Treasury of Devotion* (Arthur James 1981), p. 262.
28. Malcolm Muggeridge, *Something Beautiful for God* (Fontana 1972), p. 126.
29. Angelo Devananda, *Mother Teresa – Contemplative at the Heart of the World* (Fount 1986), p. 31.

30. ibid., p. 36.
31. ibid., p. 139.
32. See again the passages on intercession mentioned on p. 49.
33. The Word of God is always compassionate. Exodus 22.27 represents a God who says of himself: 'I AM full of compassion.' Cf. *Contemplating the Word*, pp. 52–4.
34. Cf. Jacob Boehme, *The Way to Christ* (Paulist Press and SPCK 'Classics of Western Spirituality' 1978), p. 43: 'Reclothe my soul . . . as with a new body that dwells in heaven, in which your divine power and Word that became man might dwell within it which is the Temple of your Holy Spirit that dwells in us . . . O great Love of Jesus Christ, I can do nothing but sink my desire in you. Your Word that became man is truth . . . Since you called me to come, I now come; let it happen to me according to your Word and will. Amen.' 'Dear reader,' he goes on to warn, 'if you are not in earnest . . . leave the above . . . prayer unsaid or [it] will be the judgement of God in you. You are not to misuse the Name of God.'
35. John 14.23 RSV.
36. Matthew 7.24.
37. 1 Kings 8.27–29.

Month Six: I will be an inner spring

1. See for example Alan Richardson (ed.), *Theological Word Book of the Bible* (SCM Press 1957), article on 'Water', pp. 279f.
2. Genesis 6–9.
3. 1 Peter 3.20.
4. Exodus 14.21–15.21.
5. Cf. Jeremiah 47.1–4.
6. Cf. Isaiah 8.5–8.
7. Isaiah 54.7–10.
8. Psalm 69.1.
9. Luke 12.50.
10. J. C. Fenton *Crucified with Christ* (SPCK 1961), p. 9.
11. Mark 10.38.
12. *Crucified with Christ*, p. 11.
13. Teresa of Avila *The Interior Castle* (Paulist Press and

SPCK 'Classics of Western Spirituality' 1980), p. 73.

14. E. Allison Peers *St Teresa's Complete Works* (Sheed and Ward 1963 'The New Ark Library'), p. 110. I commend a careful exploration of chapters 11–19.
15. Bath. The largest Jewish liquid measure: about six gallons.
16. Cf. 1 Kings 7.23–39.
17. Cf. Leviticus 14f.
18. Psalm 51.1, 2, 7, 10.
19. Ezekiel 36.25–6. Cf. Zechariah 13.1. Note that the words 'spring' and 'sprinkling' share the same root. In ritual cleansing, the clear, pure, living, running spring water was sprinkled, splashed, flung over the unclean person: cf. Numbers 19.13.
20. Ezekiel 47.1–12. cf. Joel 3.18: 'A fountain shall spring from the Lord's House', and Revelation 22.1: 'He showed me the river of the water of life, sparkling like crystal, flowing from the throne of God and of the Lamb.'
21. Cf. Jeremiah 2.13.
22. John 4.7–15.
23. Cf. Mark 1.4–10.
24. John 3.5.
25. Ephesians 5.26.
26. Hebrews 10.22.
27. Titus 3.5.
28. Cf. Irenaeus: 'God shapes humanity out of frail matter, with his two "hands", the Word and the Spirit.' Quoted in Jones, Wainwright & Yarnold (Eds) *The Study of Spirituality* (SPCK 1986), p. 108.
29. See Gordon S. Wakefield (ed.), *A Dictionary of Christian Spirituality* (SCM Press 1983), article 'Catharsis', p. 79; and *The Study of Spirituality*, p. 616, 'Index of Subjects' reference to 'spiritual stages' and the rich variety of authors and writers to which the references helpfully point.
30. John 15.3.
31. Exodus 17.1–7.
32. Psalms 78.15; 114.7–8. Cf. 105.41; 107.35.
33. Isaiah 41.17–18, 43.20.

34. Isaiah 44.3, 55.1–3.
35. Psalm 23.2.
36. 1 Corinthians 10.1–4.
37. John 4.14; 6.35; 7.37–8. The 'Authorised Version' of the Scriptures speaks perhaps more evocatively of the living water flowing 'out of the belly'.
38. Revelation 21.6, 22.7.
39. See for example *Theological Word Book of the Bible*, 'Waters of Fruitfulness and Refreshment' in article 'Water', p. 281.
40. Psalms 42.1, 63.1–2.
41. Many contemplatives habitually sit with hands resting lightly on the lap with palms upwards. The attitude is well explored in Henri Nouwen's *With Open Hands* (Ave Maria Press 1972), e.g.: 'Deep silence leads us to suspect that, in the first place, prayer is acceptance. A man who prays is a man . . . with his hands open to the world . . . In the silence of prayer you can spread out your hands to embrace God, your fellowman, and nature' (pp. 56, 76). Sometimes, for me at least, the 'living water' of Word and Spirit, flows and spreads out from those open hands. I commend Henri Nouwen's writings to those exploring a contemplative way of prayer and life.
42. Cf. Month 4, note 13. Cf. also John Cassian *Conferences* (Paulist Press and SPCK 'Classics of Western Spirituality' 1985), pp. 118f.
43. Catherine of Siena *The Dialogue* (Paulist Press and SPCK 'Classics of Western Spirituality' 1980), pp. 161f. I have noticed, without any prompting from me, how easily and frequently tears flow from many of those who attend the contemplative retreats I am privileged to lead. Some have said that the shedding of tears has been a new and creative experience for them. Some have spoken of being unable to shed *physical* tears but nevertheless have shed what St Catherine learns are 'tears of fire . . . which often satisfy those who want to weep but cannot.'
44. Isaiah 55.10–13.
45. Louis Evely, *Our Prayer* (Mowbray 1970), p. 118.
46. Psalm 36.8; Amos 5.24; Psalm 107.35; Isaiah 35.6–7;

49.10; 43.2. cf. Proverbs 10.11; Isaiah 11.9; Habakkuk 2.14; Revelation 1.15.
47. Isaiah 55.12–13. cf. John 15.11.
48. John Ruusbroec, *The Spiritual Espousals and other Works*, p. 184.

Appendix

1. Cf. Deuteronomy 8.3; Matthew 4.4.
2. See for example *Contemplating the Word*, pp. 52–54.
3. Jones, Wainwright and Yarnold, *The Study of Spirituality* refers to 'a state where symbols and concepts are transcended and God is known by unknowing. This is . . . the theology of rest . . . The intellect passes beyond any active knowledge, whether from the senses or by concepts, and is reduced to "complete speechlessness"' (p. 188).

CONTEMPLATING THE WORD

Peter Dodson

Peter Dodson introduces a way of contemplation for all who wish to base their spirituality on words and images drawn directly from the Bible. Here is a wealth of sound advice and encouragement, not only on the meaning and discipline of contemplation, but also on the spiritual benefits that can arise from the indwelling Word – how it can take root and grow in our minds and hearts, producing healing and wholeness in our actions, in our relationships and above all in our worship and love of God.

'Full of practical advice with holy living in view.'   *Baptist Times*

'Completely soaked in the Bible, and utterly practical.' *Fairacres Chronicle*

'It burns with love for God's word . . . there is much enrichment here.'   *Church Review*

'Easy to read and practical.'   *Leadership Today*